BATTLEFIELD ARCHAEOLOGY

BATTLEFIELD ARCHAEOLOGY

TIM LYNCH AND JON COOKSEY

TEMPUS

To Jacqueline, for feigning interest in a variety of empty fields.
To Bethany, for her love of going to history and to Joshua, who, quite
honestly, was no help whatsoever but provided the reality checks. TL

First published 2007

Tempus Publishing
Cirencester Road, Chalford,
Stroud, Gloucestershire, GL6 8PE
www.tempus-publishing.com

Tempus Publishing is an imprint of NPI Media Group

British Library Cataloguing in Publication Data.
A catalogue record for this book is available from the British Library.

ISBN 978 0 7524 4094 1

Typesetting and origination by NPI Media Group
Printed in Great Britain

CONTENTS

PREFACE

This book began life on a hot June day in Normandy. Tim Lynch's long-suffering family had been dragged around the D-Day beaches and landing sites, subjected along the way to long roving lectures about what happened on blank stretches of sand, until it ended up on the *Pointe-du-Hoc*. In this preserved memorial park was some evidence that something had happened. On 6 June 1944, this had been a German strongpoint, with artillery capable of wreaking havoc among the fleet delivering troops to the invasion beachheads. Because of its position and strength, no one could guarantee that it could be put out of action by bombing or shelling from the sea. It had to be taken by troops on the ground. American Rangers were tasked with landing below the cliff and climbing up ladders to seize the guns. Under fire all the way, they fought their way up the cliffs and captured the bunkers, holding them against fierce counter attacks until a force from nearby Omaha Beach reached them.

Despite what Tim personally considered to be a fascinating, dramatic and brilliantly delivered description of events, his family's eyes had started glazing over, so they took a break to sit on the grass and enjoy the sunshine outside of one of the old bunkers. Six-year-old Bethany suddenly noticed something on the ground beside her and picked up what turned out to be the cartridge case of a German K98 rifle round. The last person to hold it had been a frightened German soldier on the morning of 6 June 1944, trying to hold back the greatest seaborne invasion the world has ever seen. Here was a tangible and direct connection between us and one of the most momentous events in history. It wasn't an object in a glass case. Nothing stood between the Lynch family and him. History was no longer abstract.

That is what archaeology is all about. That is why archaeologists often refer to the excitement of discovering an item that has lain undisturbed since it was dropped by another human being hundreds, even thousands, of years ago. It captures the imagination in a way that even the best told history cannot. It's about real people doing real things. Certainly, in recent years it has caught the public's imagination with a whole range of archaeology-based television shows involving the public as never before. Writing about their own television series, battlefield specialists Tony Pollard and Neil Oliver admit that their reason for studying battle sites is simple, saying:

1 An archaeological imagination. Bethany Lynch with a collection of her own battlefield finds

> Let's start by being completely honest about why we started studying battlefields in the first place; this stuff can be almost too exciting for words … the experience of doing this type of archaeology is very personal, even intimate. What we are sometimes looking at when we relocate objects dropped by soldiers – the arrowheads or bullets they used in battle, for example – are the movements and actions of a person who could have been in the last hours or even moments of his life.

It is this appeal to the imagination that makes archaeology so attractive. Clive Gamble wrote 'archaeology is about excitement. It is about intellectual curiosity and finding ways to turn that curiosity into knowledge about people in the past.' Archaeology, he argues, is an act of the imagination. Indeed, Julian Thomas referred to 'our archaeological imagination' as the ability think about ourselves and our past in new and exciting ways. At one level, the archaeological imagination is really just a refinement of our taken-for-granted ability to reconstruct in our daily lives what went on from the evidence left behind – a jacket left over the back of a chair tells us that its owner will probably still be in the building; a room littered with glasses and bottles indicates that a party has taken place. It is this ability that has, over the last 200 years, developed into the science of archaeology.

Imagination is what drives archaeology and, in large part, it is only our imagination that allows us to create an image of the past. In 1927, George Trevelyan spoke of it as finding wreckage washed up on the beach and using this to recreate the ship that has gone forever. More recently, Simon Schama wrote of historians as 'forever chasing shadows, painfully aware of their inability ever to reconstruct a dead world in its completeness, however thorough or revealing their documentation … We are doomed to be forever hailing someone who has just gone around the corner and out of earshot.'

A visit to any battlefield can be an extraordinary experience. When the fighting moves on, the site slowly returns to nature – flowers grow where blood flowed, birds sing where shells shrieked. Sometimes an atmosphere hangs over the scene and no-one leaves without being affected by it. Sometimes so little remains that it is difficult to find any reason to suspect that for hours, even days, human beings experienced the most intense emotions imaginable. Historian Tim Newark said that 'trying to conceive what it was like at the time of the battle is the supreme act of imagination' (2002: 7). At the same time, it can also be incredibly dull without a will to understand, to imagine and respect those who were there on that fateful day. History is something we are all aware of – people use it all the time to justify their point of view, but few of us actually care about it enough to want to understand. The First World War is part of the National Curriculum but learning about it in a warm, dry classroom means very little. Watch a school party as they walk across a field on the Somme and you will see history, not just a subject, but as an emotion.

In this book, we will explore the study of scenes of conflict, some of them only a few years in the past. It may seem strange to talk of archaeology as a means of learning about events that are, in some cases, still within living memory, but sometimes people didn't bother to write about things because they were commonplace then. Now those memories are being lost forever. Sometimes, as with the secret bunkers prepared in readiness for the apocalyptic vision of nuclear war, records are not accessible and won't be for many years – by which time the structures themselves may be gone. Where there are no accessible sources of information, the purpose of such sites are as mysterious as those of prehistoric standing stones, and the skills of the prehistorian can be just as valid for something twenty-years old as for something 20,000 years or more. In any case, even as our heritage is becoming part of the entertainment industry, the real story is being forgotten. Myth is overtaking reality and soon all we will have is a past in which Robin Hood was American and a version of the Second World War that makes us nostalgic for the happiness and security that only rationing, Glen Miller and the threat of imminent death can bring.

This book is about using your imagination to understand the stories behind the military history that is everywhere around you. The past may be somewhere we can never really travel to, but Bethany Lynch, whose imagination does not yet have boundaries, is always eager to 'go to history'. She and her father often go there together. History has given them the precious gift of time – make of it what you will.

Tim Lynch & Jon Cooksey
May 2007

INTRODUCTION

American archaeologist Bill McMillon observed:

> The justices of the United States Supreme Court once ruled that science is what scientists do. The same can be said for archaeology. To paraphrase the justices, archaeology is what professional archaeologists say it is, and most say it is a study of things that humans have made; a study conducted by using scientific methods to systematically recover material evidence of life and culture from past ages, and make detailed investigations from that evidence. In other words, archaeologists try to reconstruct life and culture of past ages through the study of objects created by humans, known as artefacts (1991: 10).

In his excellent introduction to the subject, Clive Gamble defines archaeology even more simply as 'basically about three things: objects, landscapes and what we make of them. It is quite simply the study of the past through material remains'. It achieves this through the use of a wide range of skills and disciplines that each contribute to the creation of a holistic image of the people and places that feature in the events that have shaped the present. The aim of battlefield archaeology, then, is to search for the evidence that will enable us to piece together the story of ordinary people caught up in war and to understand it in terms of the impact it has on their lives and environment.

Although there is general agreement about what the aim of archaeology is, battlefield archaeology is a specialism and, as with any specialist field, whenever a group of experts gather, the first area of disagreement will inevitably be about what it is that they are expert in. Battlefield archaeologists are no different. Tim Sutherland, whose ongoing work on the battlefield at Towton has placed him at the forefront of British research, suggests that the term 'Battlefield Archaeology' can be misleading as a description of what is actually being undertaken. Battlefield archaeology, he argues, generally focuses on the archaeology of specific events, such as the battle, rather than the actual field on which it took place. Alternatively, 'the archaeology of battle' is therefore often used as a more precise description of the aim of the study. That, too, can be misleading, in that attempting to understand the archaeology of a battle can lead to channeling research into perhaps one particular event rather than recognising that such actions may be repeated over time. For example, the medieval battlefield of Formigny lies a short distance inland from the beaches used on D-Day – medieval relics and twentieth-century artefacts are both likely to surface in the same fields. Consequently, Sutherland writes that the 'archaeology of battle' should instead form part of a 'battlefield project' which recognises this use and reuse of land. Equally, the methods and skills applied to battlefield archaeology lend themselves to other incidents of organised violence. Michael Rayner, of the Battlefields Trust (2005), has included Luddite violence in the mills of Yorkshire among his listing of English battlefields, and Sutherland himself points to the 'Peterloo Massacre' as an example where the application of archaeological techniques to an investigation of skeletal trauma could be used to deny or confirm contemporary accounts of incidents of civil conflict. He concludes that yet another term, 'the "archaeology of conflict", rather than "battlefield archaeology", is therefore a more appropriate general expression.' (2005: 1–2).

In this book, the term 'battlefield archaeology' is used because that is the most widely understood description of what is being undertaken, but we use it in its widest sense to refer to any attempt to systematically study evidence of military activity. As such, it encompasses the 'archaeology of conflict' at both the macro and micro level. With genealogy rapidly expanding as a hobby, it is argued that a fading snapshot of granddad in uniform is as much an artefact of battlefield archaeology as the rusting relic recovered from a professional excavation, and should be treated as such.

This, then, is also a book about battlefield archaeology aimed primarily at people without formal training in the relevant disciplines. Many professional academics would argue that a book like this should not be put down lightly – it should be hurled aside with as much abuse as possible. The popularisation of archaeology through television over recent years has not been universally welcomed, especially by those who have not been invited before the cameras. The public, they say, should fund archaeology, but the work should be left to professionals. Ironically, for a profession whose origins lie in the amateur explorations of sites of interest, there is a belief that history is too important to be entrusted to amateurs. There is some truth to that.

Any sort of archaeology, and battlefield archaeology, in particular, is exciting. The availability of affordable metal detecting equipment can turn anyone into a tomb-raiding weekend Indiana Jones or Lara Croft. This is where the problems start. The context in which an object is found is what makes it important and it is this context which helps us to understand how something was used and why. A musket ball or arrowhead might be an interesting souvenir but once picked up it tells us nothing of the circumstances surrounding how it came to be there. Imagine a simple fingerprint. A fingerprint on a piece of pipe means nothing, but a fingerprint on a piece of pipe found at a murder scene is hugely important. That is why professional archaeologists are so concerned with the struggle to preserve sites from the casual souvenir hunter. Without understanding how a find is linked to the site, we can learn nothing from it.

Despite the faint aroma of sour grapes from those who condemn populist archaeology, there is a real and genuine concern about the potential damage to our heritage of enthusiastic amateurs setting out on their own excavations and accidentally harming the

Starting bid   £5.00   [Place Bid >]

End time: **23-Jun-06 20:06:24 BST** (5 days 8 hours)

Postage costs: **£3.00** Royal Mail 1st Class Standard

Post to: Worldwide

Item location: Newbury, United Kingdom

History: 0 bids

You can also: Watch this item
    Email to a friend

Listing and payment details: Show

Seller: _____ (579 ★)
Feedback: **100% Positive**
Member: since 30-Jan-01 in United Kingdom
   Read feedback comments
   Ask seller a question
   Add to Favourite Sellers
   View seller's other items

Buy safely

1. **Check the seller's reputation**
Score: 579 | 100% Positive
Read feedback comments

2. **Learn how you are protected**
PayPal Buyer Protection
   Free Coverage now up to £500. See eligibility.

Description (revised)   Seller assumes all responsibility for listing this item

Item Specifics
   Condition: **Used**

2 Musket balls for sale on the Internet. Sales like these can cause immense damage to the information that can be gathered from unprotected sites

evidence in their hurry to unearth treasures of the past. There are also concerns about the ever-growing market for artefacts supplied by unscrupulous 'nighthawks', metal-detectorists who plunder sites for anything worth selling on the worldwide antiquities market. There are tales of bin bags of bones being dumped outside police stations around the towns along what was once known as the Western Front – in them the remains of First World War soldiers found in the fields of Flanders and stripped of anything worth selling, as well as evidence that may identify the body and allow a family some peace. The nighthawks who dump these bones, sadly, are the more respectful of their kind – many don't even show a degree of decency and simply throw the bones back into the ground.

The battle lines have been drawn between, on the one hand a small clique of highly trained specialists who want to keep the public as far away from their work as possible, and on the other those members of the public who want to make a fast profit from the antiquities market. In between these extremes lie the vast majority of us – the great many archaeologists and researchers who are passionate about their work and eager to share it with others at any opportunity and members of the public who are just as eager to learn. The central theme of this book is about how to get actively involved in the field of conflict archaeology as an amateur, without the risk of causing harm to the work of the professionals.

WHY STUDY BATTLEFIELDS?

There are many reasons for researching fields of conflict, but perhaps the main one is a willingness to remember the true cost of war. Each year since the mid-1980s, the

US government has sent ten expeditions per year into Southeast Asia to search for the remains of missing American soldiers and airmen. Other teams search Korea, others the Pacific, Europe and anywhere where US personnel served. The Central Identification Laboratory, Hawaii (CILHI) is part of Joint Task Force-Full Accounting, a $100 million a year operation, unprecedented in military history, dedicated to recovering any identifiable remains, however small, so that families can finally say goodbye to their loved ones (Swift 2003). By contrast, every year in northern France, the remains of men who died in the mud of the Western Front emerge, sometimes brought to light by the plough, sometimes by bulldozer and only rarely by people looking for them. Most are reburied in anonymous graves but each was once a human being as Alistair Fraser (2005) ably demonstrated when the skeleton of 'German No.1', uncovered during an archaeological dig near Serre on the Somme, was identified as Jakob Hönes, allowing him the dignity of a marked grave and 14 members of his family to attend his funeral nearly 90 years after he died. The same year, in Latvia, a volunteer expedition uncovered the remains of no fewer than 160 Russian soldiers in a single expedition, all of whom were, like hundreds of others, buried in a mass grave by the Russian government in an official ceremony, held annually each May, to inter that year's crop of war dead (Sogndal 2004).

Across the world, battlefield archaeology ranges in its scope and resources from the multi-million dollar governmental search for war dead to the work of individuals funding research from their own pockets to commemorate one incident or an individual. Whether it is conducted by a professional team searching for a single bone fragment from which to extract DNA on behalf of a single family, or by a volunteer team unearthing mass burials, or even simply a project to acknowledge that here is a spot of some significance to history, for those involved, the aim is the same – to acknowledge the impact of war on human life and remember that this is what lies behind the nameless thousands who make up the formations whose names appear in the history books. Most of all, though, battlefield archaeology is about remembering that wars are fought by real people and about finding out what that experience was like for those who took part.

However noble the aim, anyone who chooses to study military conflict as a hobby runs the risk of being regarded as a bit of a social misfit with quite a pathetic interest in war for its excitement and thrills. John Schofield, head of Military Programmes for English Heritage and lecturer in archaeology, describes having been invited to be interviewed on a radio station about his work in defence heritage projects, for what he then heard the presenter call 'Anorak Hour'. There is an assumption that anoraks who like military history are somehow inadequates who are excited by vicarious heroism. By contrast, oddly enough, young men who read any and every book about various SAS exploits, and play at being soldiers on computer games, are regarded as perfectly normal.

Equally, the student of conflict is likely, at some point, to be accused of glorifying war simply by being interested in its causes and effects. Each year as the annual Armistice Day commemorations of the nation's war dead approaches, the media revives the debate around whether we should forget the past and move on. Certainly there are arguments in favour of a more forward looking approach, but Britain remains firmly entrenched in a memory of its former glories that shows no sign of fading.

3 Nostalgia for the Second World War can cloud our understanding of what it meant for so many people

Anthropologists talk of the importance of myth in any culture as a means of understanding the past and present. Myths are not, as often assumed, 'lies'. They are simply shared beliefs about the history of a society that influence its response to any new situation. In the UK, a huge 'heritage' industry has grown up around the collective myths of the Second World War and they pervade almost every aspect of our daily lives from football matches to nostalgic television programmes to news and current affairs. In reporting on British troops in action from the Falklands to the Gulf, journalists have had to rely on these shared ideas to convey their stories to an audience with no military experience beyond these myths. So powerful is the influence of these assumed memories that in 2007, with British troops being killed in action in Iraq and Afghanistan, the British public still talk of 1945 as the end of 'the last war'.

George Santayana famously argued that 'those who cannot remember the past are condemned to repeat it'. What, then, of the event organised to commemorate the anniversary of the end of the Second World War which offered the chance to 'relive the good old days of the 1940s'? One wonders whether those, who remember from first-hand experience the fear of hearing the drone of German V1 and V2 rockets and the wait for the engine to stop as the bombs fell to earth, would really be as enthusiastic about 'a night of jitterbugs and doodlebugs' as the bloodless generations who have only experienced a sanitised and nostalgic myth of life in wartime.

At the start of a new millennium, you might expect people to look to the future and what the next 1000 years may bring. Instead, in an insecure world, we are turning more and more to the comfort of the past when the world was a safer, more certain place. An entire heritage industry has developed to feed the appetite for an understanding of who we are and where we come from. The search for an identity is at the root of the growth of genealogy to become one of the most popular pastimes today. But what is 'history'? It has been described by Paul Valery as:

> ... the most dangerous substance that the chemistry of the intellect has created ... It makes men dream, it intoxicates them, breeds false memories in them, aggravates their responses, takes up their ancient grievances, torments them in their sleep, carries them into the delirium of grandeur or else of persecution, and turns nations bitter, intolerable and vain (1928:45).

It has been called 'the story of our past' by social anthropologists searching for clues about ideas of nationhood and identity, and more often than not what we see as 'history' defines not who we are, but who we would like to be. After all, it is always written by the winners. History is not a lake, fixed, still and unchanging. It is a river, always shifting and always with something new to reveal.

In recent years, a debate has developed among Living History re-enactors – whose hobby involves presenting historical displays to the public – about why so few people from minority groups chose to join in such activities, or even attend these displays. At the centre of this debate is a tacit understanding that 'British' history really means 'white' history. Yet for those who study military history, the idea of multicultural Britain as a product of the late twentieth century can soon be dispelled. We know, for example, that Roman garrisons in north-east England were manned by troops from what is now Iraq nearly 2000 years ago. It is entirely likely that some will have served out their time in the legions before settling down in Britain. We also know that the Vikings traded with India and North Africa, and that the strong probability exists of black and Asian warriors being part of Viking raids and armies throughout the Dark Ages. London's National Army Museum holds a painting of a cavalry charge during the Thirty Years' War (1618-38) in which a black cavalryman can be clearly seen riding with his white comrades. When Nelson's flagship *Victory* sailed into the French and Spanish fleets at Trafalgar in a crowning moment of British history, it carried aboard 441 Englishmen, sixty-four Scots, sixty-three Irish, eighteen Welsh, three Shetlanders, two Channel Islanders, one Manxman, twenty-one Americans, seven Dutch, six Swedes, four Italians, four Maltese, three Norwegians, three Germans, two Swiss, two Portuguese, two Danes, two Indians, one Russian, one Brazilian, one African, nine West Indians and three French volunteers (Adkins 2004:50). At least one painting of Nelson's death features a black sailor and his plinth in Trafalgar Square has a black sailor carved among his white crewmates. At Waterloo, former slave George Rose was wounded and later received the Waterloo Medal, ending his Army career as a sergeant. In 1857, William Hall became the first black man to be awarded the newly instituted Victoria Cross during the Indian Mutiny. And so the list goes on. The battlefield can be a very cosmopolitan place, and studying them can tell us a lot about some surprising attitudes to race over the years, if we take the time to find out.

4 In France, as in Britain, nationalist history has largely ignored the contribution of colonial forces. Here, French African soldiers are held as POWs by the Germans, France 1940. *Tim Lynch collection*

For those of us born since, the Second World War can seem like ancient history – remote and removed from our world today. Yet the past is never as far away as we think. On 19 December 1959, Walter Williams, the last known veteran of the American Civil War, died. Gertrude Janeway, who married Union veteran John in 1927 when she was 18 and he 81, died in January 2003. The last surviving widow of a Confederate soldier of the American Civil War, Alberta Martin, died as recently as May 2004. A war which took place over 140 years ago is only two lifetimes away. There is a widely held belief that we are separated from everyone else on the planet by only 'six degrees of separation' – you have met someone, who has met someone, who has met someone and so on, until you reach your target. That is here, and now. The archaeological imagination allows us to turn the process slightly around.

Just as the finding of a German cartridge case made D-Day immediate to the Lynch family, so too you can make the battles of history personal. It's simply a question of mathematics. Let's assume that you are an only child. Your parents were also the only children of their respective parents and so on. Then let's assume that a generation is the time it takes for a child to grow and have children of its own – say, 30 years. In one generation you have two ancestors, in two generations you have four, in three you have eight. So, as Bill Bryson points out in his *A Short History of Nearly Everything*, one only needs to go back a few generations for these numbers to start adding up. At eight generations, say around 1850, there are 250 ancestors. Two centuries further back and that number has risen to 16,384 people. Bryson said:

At twenty generations the number of people procreating on your behalf has risen to 1,048,576. Five generations before that, and there are no fewer than 33,554,432 men and women on whose devoted couplings your existence depends … remember, these aren't cousins and aunts and other incidental relatives, but only parents and parents of parents in a line leading ineluctably to you (2004: 480-1).

Remember, too, that we have set the time span of a generation at thirty years, less than half the allotted 'three score and ten' we might expect to live. By this token, the English Civil War of 350 years ago – when it is estimated that one in four males were directly involved and thus around 2000 male ancestors of yours were caught up in some form of fighting – is comfortably within the lifetime of you and four or five direct ancestors. The battles of history matter because, in all probability, an ancestor of yours was involved and if an arrow had moved just a fraction on a battlefield 700 years ago, you would not be who you are today.

If we chose, we can make the past relevant to today yet most do not choose to do so. In the preface to his 1950 *The Battlefields of England*, A.H. Burne described how he had set out to write a guide for the 'intelligent inhabitants of this land' to aide their appreciation of the importance of English battlefields. He said:

As my researches proceeded I became increasingly aware of the fact that this aspect of our national history has been surprisingly – even shockingly – neglected and disregarded during the present century. The ignorance that exists today, not only among the educated public, but also among those whose duty it is to hand on the knowledge, is deplorable.

Over half a century later, in 2005, Portsmouth hosted 'Trafalgar 200', a multinational event to commemorate the bicentennial anniversary of perhaps one of the most famous battles in British history. Reporters talking to people in the crowd found that many, even some who claimed to have studied history and gained qualifications in it, were unable to give the date of the battle or even the year it took place, despite the clue in the title of the event.

Britain as a nation has been defined by its military past and yet for the most part we neither know, nor care, about learning from it. A visit to the military history section of any bookshop will reveal hundreds of studies of battles and soldiers, but the fact remains that we know an awful lot about not very much. Most of the titles you will find will be about the Nazis or D-Day. You will be hard pressed to find any account of the British invasion of Madagascar or the Allied landings in southern France. These are battles in which people died but which remain, as one editor put it, 'not famous enough to be of interest'.

Even those battles that do achieve the status of celebrity combats are rarely as clear-cut as we sometimes assume. Foard (2005), for example, has shown that the thousands of words dedicated to describing the battle of Naseby, during the English Civil War, have consistently misplaced the battlelines. Archaeological evidence from the distribution of musketballs has shown that the accepted version of events are wrong.

Sir Winston Churchill wrote that battles were 'the punctuation marks of history', and we can view battlefields as the pages on which history has been written. They represent the sites on which pivotal moments in our history have occurred, where the skills and techniques that forged an empire were developed and refined, where great leaders have demonstrated their abilities.

Sir Jocelyn Stevens, a former Chairman of English Heritage, has recognised the significance of battlefield sites and has said that '[e]very battlefield is a testament to unknown soldiers who fought and died in the making of Britain's history. It is vital that those battlefields that still remain should be recognised and should survive.' Despite this, by 2005 only forty-three battlefields are on the English Heritage register and only one piece of research – the report that underpinned the register itself – has been funded by English Heritage. At present, the only real sources of funding for battlefield research are television companies.

One of the main reasons for studying conflict, then, is simply to remember where, how and why members of our families died in the thousands of battles, sieges and skirmishes that punctuate history. There are some 36,000 memorials across the UK to the First World War alone and it is claimed that since its foundation in 1650, the British Army has had only one 12-month period (between late 1968 and 1969) in which it has not suffered the death of a soldier in action. On those thousands of memorials are the names of local people who fought and died in places they had never heard of, for a cause they often could not fully explain because they were sent there to do just that. Each was a real person with family and friends and hopes for the future. Each name deserves to be remembered, not as a glorious hero, but as a human being. Few who study war seriously see it as glamorous. Sometimes wars are the result of mistakes. Sometimes they are a necessary evil. Very rarely wars are a means of improving the lives of others. The study of how and why we fight can help us to learn to tell the difference.

WHAT IS THERE TO STUDY?

Britain is a landscape defined by war. In the twentieth century alone, it is estimated that by 1944 20 per cent of the land surface of the UK was under some form of military control (Foot 2002). By 1945, there were some 750 airfields of various types and between 1939 and 1945 an estimated five aircraft per day crashed somewhere in the country (de la Bédoyère 2001: 8). Osborne (2004) reports an unknown number of concrete pillboxes (thought to have been over 28,000) and the Cold War era added a further 1,500 bunkers to the list, possibly more. New sites remain to be uncovered, sometimes in the unlikeliest places. On 23 March 2006, *The Independent* newspaper reported the discovery of a nuclear defence bunker in the foundations of the Brooklyn Bridge in central New York. A worker for the city's Department of Transportation had noticed the door during a maintenance inspection and decided to push it open. Inside he found medical kits, blankets and even boxes of crackers, stored there since 1962 and long forgotten. John Lewis Gaddis, an expert on the era at Yale University, described it as an archaeological find, in the sense of having discovered artefacts of a period of real threat of war. Kay Sarlin, a spokeswoman for the city, admitted that they simply didn't know it was there and that there may be many more such time capsules waiting to be found. In many ways, the Cold War and its attendant secrecy makes the study of even our most recent past as difficult a task as interpreting prehistoric monuments. Because it is so recent, there is a very real risk that by the time it seems worth recording as history, the evidence will be gone.

Despite the growing number of professionals working in the field, an enormous amount of work remains that can be usefully undertaken by amateurs working at a local level either alone or in groups. In recent years, for example, the Defence of Britain Project (Schofield 2005: 56-8) used teams of volunteers to catalogue the neglected remnants of the anti-invasion defences hurriedly put in place to counter the threat of German assault in 1940. Between 1995 and 2002 over 13,000 sites were recorded (Osborne 2004). Without the aid of volunteers, this work could not have been completed. In London, a Community Archaeology Project has begun work on excavating homes destroyed in the bombings of the Blitz (Museum of London 2006) using official documents, eyewitness testimony and archaeological evidence to uncover life in wartime London.

Grant, Gorin and Fleming (2002) report that there are some 15,000 sites of archaeological significance listed and given some measure of protection as monuments under the National Heritage Act 1983 in the UK. However, this represents only around 2 per cent of the total number of known sites. The British countryside is quite literally littered with remnants of conflict. Taking just one example of a relatively small area of the country, Mervyn Jones (2000) wrote about the development of the South Yorkshire landscape. In an area of 603sq.m. (roughly 24.5 miles x 24.5 miles) he identified:

1 8 Iron Age hillforts
2 4 existing Roman forts and another known to have been destroyed by building work
3 13 motte and bailey forts built in the aftermath of the Norman invasion
4 3 stone keep castles
5 30 fortified houses

His list stops there but we can reliably add at least:

1 3 battlesites
2 4 sieges
3 Nineteenth-century army and militia barracks at Sheffield, Doncaster, Barnsley and Rotherham
4 Airfields around Doncaster from the earliest Royal Flying Corps interceptor fields built to defend the area from zeppelin raids to a nuclear bomber field
5 Practice trenches dug by the men of the Sheffield Battalions in training for the Somme
6 Anti-invasion defences built in 1940, including a pillbox incorporated into a house cellar

5 At the entrance to a business park, a derelict Churchill tank acts as the only memorial to the armament factory that once stood here and built the tanks that landed on D-Day

7   Armament factories including the area in which the famous Bailey Bridge was developed

8   'Blitz' damage in all the major towns

9   Aircraft crash sites including that of a B17 bomber on the outskirts of Sheffield

10   A WW2 prisoner of war camp for captured officers

Even a conservative estimate produces one military-related site for every 2.6 miles travelled within the county. Travel only a very short distance beyond the boundaries of South Yorkshire and the castles of Pontefract and Sandal add a history of warfare from the Wars of the Roses to the Civil War. To the south, the villages between Tickhill and Bawtry were once part of an official tournament area. Knights would train for battle by rampaging across this stretch of countryside, using it as a medieval equivalent of the way the modern army uses Salisbury Plain.

It is sometimes easy to assume that in a country so rich in history everything that needs to be researched has been studied. The fact is, as we have already seen, we only know about those battles famous enough to pass the publisher's test of whether it will sell. A book on D-Day will sell because all the others have. The problem is that famous battles are, by their very status, unusual events. That is why they are remembered and written about. Most soldiers have never fought in one. Battles, by definition, are planned events in which both sides prepare and manoeuvre. By contrast, most fighting takes place in unplanned encounters or skirmishes – by far the more common experience of soldiering. Writing of the English Civil Wars, Philip Tennant argued that it is impossible to fully understand the events of the English Civil War because relatively few of those caught up in events had the literacy skills or opportunity to create a permanent record. Just as the stories of hundreds of thousands of Britons who experienced the Second World War will soon be lost because they are seen as so commonplace that they are not worth recording, so, too, were accounts of the ordinary people in conflicts throughout history. In the English Civil War, major battles were recorded but not the day to day raids and skirmishes that were by far the more common experience. Tennant wrote:

> … one should beware of parish histories which tend to assume that because a village's name is absent from a particular archive the war must have passed it by untouched, for it is unlikely to have been so … for every single event recorded countless others were not. The testimony of that scholarly eyewitness Richard Baxter is both significant and authoritative: 'I think there were very few Parishes where at one time or another Blood has not been shed'. (1992: xii)

A brief survey of any area of the UK will unearth some form of military activity during the past 2000 years, if not before. Sometimes it may be only the weathered remains of a hillfort used to defend against local cattle raiders and soon abandoned. Sometimes there is evidence of prolonged use, such as Pevensey Castle, where a Second World War gun emplacement sits among ruins of the Roman defences. Sometimes it may be as simple as a Commonwealth War Grave headstone in a parish church, but always there is a story to be found.

6 The overgrown commemoration on the family of Thomas Sutton, a First World War soldier who died in Cambridge from the effects of a gas attack in France. Men like Sutton are today largely forgotten and ignored. Without understanding what they went through, we cannot understand how their lives and deaths shaped the modern world

What follows is not a textbook and makes no pretence to be. Instead, it is intended as a guide to the process of conducting research into the military past. In the following chapters we will look at what battlefield archaeology is and why it is relevant today, at what sort of research is taking place and how to undertake a project, from identification of sources of information to preparing a final report. We will explore what Paul Hill and Julie Wileman (2002) have called 'the landscapes of war' – the interaction between the landscape and the military. We will look at landscapes of defence and how static castles and bunkers have been used for millennia to control areas of ground and how they continue to do so. We will focus on landscapes of offence and how earthworks, trenches and foxholes have been used to aid the attack. We will also see how the landscape has changed and at how it has remained as it was on that fateful day and how this can help us to understand events and decisions that were made. Debate between historians and archaeologists about their respective roles rumbles on in papers and books, read with varying degrees of interest by those who write them and those whose course requires them to read. Is archaeology 'the handmaiden of history' or is it the primary approach to recovering evidence of the lives of our ancestors and therefore leading our understanding of history? The answer is not in this book. In this book, 'archaeology' is used in its widest possible sense to describe the whole process of piecing together the story of a battlefield and the people who fought there. To really understand the events that took place hundreds of years ago, we need to have as much information as possible at our disposal – from books, maps, stories, and from the ground before us and objects beneath it.

We will start from the first steps of designing a research plan to the use of documents, maps and oral history, the problems of locating a battlesite today and of recovering artefacts. We shall explore the resources available to the amateur with little time and no funding and at what can still be achieved. Using examples of current research, we will see how the story of a battle can be uncovered and interpreted. Most of all, this book is simply about the pleasure and satisfaction to be gained by unlocking and using our archaeological imagination.

I

LANDSCAPES OF CONFLICT

To say that landscape affects military operations is to state the obvious. Paul Hill and Julie Wileman have pointed out that once forms of organised warfare become recognisable within any form of human society, its relationship to the practical factors of landscape and climate become equally recognisable. Decisions about attack and defence are inextricably linked with the dictates of the geology, vegetation, land use and climate of the region. The problems of moving troops over recently ploughed, wet clay soil are very different to those of advancing across a dry meadow. These are factors that can determine the weapons, tactics, supply, transport, fortifications and strategy. The Western Front of the First World War is always associated with the digging of trenches but in some cases, the soil conditions were such that digging in would have sunk the trenches below the water table and immediately flooded them so that instead, defences had to be built up from ground level. These are the kind of issues that link landscape and war. In archaeological terms, though, a landscape is far more complex than a simple arrangement of hills and valleys. 'Equally inseparable are cognitive elements of landscape recognitions – the perceptions of sacredness, ownership and land potential, ancestral roots and meaning, wealth and status exemplified by control or access to specific territories and regions.' (Hill & Wileman 2002: 14).

So what is it? What, for example, does Schofield (2005) mean when he writes of the 'bomber landscape' of East Anglia? The European Landscape Convention (Fairclough and Rippon 2002) defines a 'landscape' as meaning 'an area, as perceived by people, whose character is the result of the action and interaction of natural and/or human factors'. Landscapes, in the sense we are using the term here, are not simply a matter of geography, it is the way that geography is perceived by the people who live there. Equally, the physical features of a landscape change very slowly but the way people use those features can change even from generation to generation – what might have been a key position in the anti-invasion defences scattered across the countryside of 1940 is today's graffiti-covered concrete eyesore in a national park. In other words, we need to think about 'battlefields', not just as the site on which a battle took place, but as part of a much broader landscape of conflict – 'why did the battle take place there and not over there?' The Bloody Meadows Project, for example, has attempted to gain an understanding of why battles were fought where they were by considering how landscape was viewed

7 Battle debris, Falkland Islands. It has been said that archaeology is a load of old rubbish, and this is what they mean. It has a lot to say about what weapons were used here and how they reached the frontlines – assuming the right questions are being asked

in strategic terms by contemporary society. It has sought to explore why battles and skirmishes took place and what factors determined that it would be the site of a battle. What were the social, economic and political effects of the fighting on the local people? It has also tried to consider how the memory of a particular battle has come down to us (Harrington 2004: 89).

At the same time, we need to think of battlefield landscapes as being located across time, too. Battles themselves may last only hours but their repercussions can be felt for centuries after the last survivor has died. Schofield's 'bomber landscape' is thus a recognition of the massive impact over time on a rural agricultural society of a sudden influx of technology, a loss of arable land beneath concrete runways and a surge of relatively affluent, often foreign, personnel into the local population. Between 1942 and 1945, East Anglia saw itself transformed into a landscape dominated by US Air Force bases where massive bomber formations took off and landed alongside fields where horses were still the main power source. Over half a century later, the impact is still being felt in the tourism, marketing and heritage industries of the area. It is felt in the social links between local families and the daughters who left with their American husbands and in the continuing presence of US bombers. Likewise, Saunders (2002) argues that northern France has become a 'multi-vocal landscape' of memorialisation, pilgrimage, heritage development and tourism centred on the events of the First World War, whilst the entire region of Normandy is developed as a vast open-air museum with guided routes set out to allow visitors to follow the progress of the invasion. These are landscapes shaped and defined by the battles that took place there.

This approach to viewing landscape as an interaction between geography, people and events allows us to think more multi-dimensionally about what 'battlefields' actually are. Michael Rayner of the Battlefields Trust (2004) has produced a record of over 500 'battles' in the UK alone, ranging from epic struggles at Hastings and Naseby to virtually unheard of incidents, such as a skirmish at Bossenden Wood in May 1838 between troops of the 45th Foot and the followers of cult leader John Thom – an action that resulted in the death of the first officer to die in action during Victoria's reign. Whatever their duration or scale, battles tend to be transient affairs, passing over ground in a matter of days, hours or even minutes, leaving in their trail the physical scars of war that gradually fade into the landscape. Battlefields, then, are the sites within the wider landscapes in which these struggles take place and where we can expect to find material evidence of their having taken place in the form of monuments and artefacts. We need to think of them as part of the whole country and as a product of the history that preceded them, rather than as an event confined within narrow physical or temporal boundaries. Perhaps this is best illustrated by considering the landscape of what has become known as the Battle of Britain.

Between early July and late October 1940, the British Royal Air Force and the German *Luftwaffe* fought for control of the skies over Britain as the threat of invasion from occupied France grew. The battle is remembered as an aerial struggle dominated by dogfights over southern England and the bombing of London and other UK cities. So can an air battle be said to have taken place on a battlefield?

The British air defence system in 1940 relied on a network of radar stations supported by Royal Observer Corps posts passing information to fighter command headquarters and squadron bases around the country. They were defended by barrage balloons designed to ensnare low-flying aircraft and by anti-aircraft artillery. Literally thousands of aircraft crashed to earth in those few months. Towns and cities were heavily bombed. So great was the effort to prevent this that sometimes more casualties were caused by the anti-aircraft fire (Hayward 2003: 71) than by enemy action. A fully-loaded *Spitfire* carried 300 rounds of ammunition for each of its eight .303 machine guns, and each used cartridge case would be ejected through ports on the wings as it was fired. In every attack, a *Spitfire*, flying at its top speed of 364mph and firing all 2400 rounds, could scatter bullet cases across miles of British countryside. If we are to think of battlefields as having taken place in the landscape, we need to consider just how much of the physical landscape of southern England contains monuments (the airfields, radar stations, anti-aircraft sites and other defence works) and artefacts (crash wreckage, shell cases, bomb splinters, and unexploded bombs) of that fighting and thus becomes, by definition, a 'battlefield'. So powerful is this perception of a 'blitz landscape' that it is the immediate point of reference for any media coverage of terrorist attacks in the city of London and it is to the 'blitz spirit' that any response is directed. Thus, the battle of Britain's battlefield landscape covers virtually the whole country and nearly 70 years.

Danger | Danger
Entrée interdite | No entry
Munitions | Undetonated
non éclatées | explosives

8 Signs around the Canadian Memorial at Vimy Ridge graphically show why unauthorised metal detecting is discouraged along the lines of the Western Front

9 A mural in Normandy commemorates the siting of a Typhoon base there in 1944. By carefully observing the local hedges and fields, elements of the base can still be found

The Duke of Wellington once famously observed that one may as well try to tell the story of a dance as of a battle. Yet for the observer, both can offer a great deal of information on the social, political and economic environment in which they take place, simply by looking at who is there and who is not, at how they interact or how they shun each other. In his analysis of the Yorkshire gentry during the English Civil War, for example, J.T. Cliffe (1969) notes that in the West Riding, 125 families declared for the king, whilst only 54 were for Parliament. Significantly, though, 110 families remained neutral. The military operations that took place within the county were not simply about one side defeating the other. They were also about a struggle for control of power and resources of those who chose to remain neutral. In that context, the large battles that took place are less significant than the campaign of raid and counter-raid that formed the overwhelming majority of military action of the time. Peter Harrington notes that most attention has been given to known battlesites and surviving siege defences, but argues that 'more work needs to be focussed upon the role of the country houses in their role as garrisoned strongholds during the war. Similarly, churches played a significant part as fortified outposts, while bridges were also equipped with defences. Research into both would extend our knowledge of fortified places' (2004: 12). These fortified houses, owned and managed by the local gentry, offer us a unique opportunity to examine the wider context of the war. These social factors are also crucial to understanding how military commanders view terrain as part of a much wider strategic, tactical, social, political and economic landscape. Following from Harrington, for example, we can view the little known battle at Tankersley Moor in 1643 as both a military necessity in clearing the way for Newcastle to move his artillery train south but also as a logistically sound investment in securing a source of iron for weapons and ammunition. Against this military background, the involvement of an active local commander, Francis Wortley, who coincidentally had interests in the manufacture of iron in the area and who had fortified two houses in a position to control the ironstone mining pits near the battlefield, highlights this need to explore more widely the reasons why people fight battles. In this case, Wortley had enthusiastically been at the forefront of the king's Army since York and dominated the land around his home for months, raising taxes for the royalist cause and generally being a pain in the neck for the local population. By another lucky coincidence, he had used his time on the Edgehill campaign to seize property belonging to Parliamentarian members of his own family and to recruit the metallurgist Dudd Dudley as his second-in-command, leaving him in a potentially very strong economic position if the war went well (see chapter ten). The study of battles sometimes requires adopting a broadly Marxist style of analysis to examine why people in such positions of power would wish to pay the economic cost in terms of personal risk, loss of workforce, upkeep of troops and, in civil war, the emotional costs of fighting within families, along with all the other expenses and losses involved, unless the potential gains were significantly higher. We need to examine the actions of any war, but particularly of the Civil War, with these factors very much in mind. Why pay the cost?

In 1914, German forces swept into France and Belgium and, in what became known as the 'race for the sea', German and Allied armies each tried to outflank the other, until they literally reached the coast and had to settle down into a stalemate that would hold for the next four years. Both sides dug in along a front that stretched from the dunes of the Belgian coast to the Swiss border. Separated in places by only a few metres of mud, two different landscapes emerged. The Germans, having occupied over 19,000 square miles of France, needed only to hold this land to claim some form of victory. To do so, they dug deep. German defences along the Western Front provided a far greater degree of protection than those of the Allies facing them. German policy was one of defence. By contrast, in order to claim victory, the Allies had to reclaim the lost land and could not be encouraged to see their lines as anything but temporary. A marked difference emerged between the two front lines. In 1916, this difference in policy was taken to its extreme when German General von Falkenhayn realised the enormous political significance of the otherwise largely redundant French fortress at Verdun, and attacked, capturing part of the complex. Militarily, it was not a strategic objective but von Falkenhayn knew that the French could not countenance its loss. At Verdun, the aim was not to break through the French lines, it was, in von Falkenhayn's words, 'to bleed France dry'. In the coming months, 400,000 French and 355,000 German soldiers would suffer on a battlefield that offered, mainly, a symbolic purpose.

10 Many homes and buildings were fortified during the Civil Wars to protect the owners from attack by either side. These towers at Houndhill in south Yorkshire are a visible reminder of those times

LANDSCAPES OF DEFENCE

In July 1940, Hitler issued 'Directive No. 16', outlining plans for Operation Sea Lion, the amphibious invasion of England. It specifically called for the use of artillery support, demanding that the largest possible number of heavy artillery units to be placed so that they could be brought into effective action as speedily as possible to protect the flanks of the invasion fleet against naval counterattack by the British and to allow counter-battery fire to be directed against shore-based guns in England. Hitler ordered the heaviest guns to be emplaced under concrete protection opposite the Straits of Dover so that they would be proof against even the heaviest air attacks and could command the Straits and prevent any movement of ships in the channel (Hitler 1940). The coastal fortifications around Calais were therefore intended to be used to protect the invasion force on its crossing and effectively project landpower outwards into the littoral (Fleming 1957: 275). When the invasion was called off, those guns not transferred to the Russian Front were given permanent concrete protection and, as the original directive had ordered, served to dominate shipping in the channel. No longer able to support offensive operations, they became the first defensive elements of the Atlantic Wall (Kaufman 2003: 195).

Later, Hitler's 'Directive No. 40' of 23 March 1942 ordered work to begin on what became known as the Atlantic Wall of 'Fortress Europe', an unbroken defensive line stretching from Norway to the Bay of Biscay. The Führer's hero, Frederick the Great, had once written that 'he who defends everything defends nothing', but the enormous initial success of the German forces had seen it conquer huge tracts of land across Europe which now needed to be held. In Russia, the German Army held a front covering over 2000km; across the Mediterranean another 4000km and from the Bay of Biscay to the Dutch coast it was held against the Anglo-American forces along 6000km of coastline. Its best troops had been decimated in actions on the Russian front and reinforcements were increasingly difficult to find.

For the next two years work would continue to create a massive barrier of concrete bunkers, trenches and artillery casemates with the aim of smashing any invasion attempt either on the beaches or immediately inland. Field Marshal Erwin Rommel, the man tasked with defending France, firmly believed that any invasion would have to be destroyed on the beaches to prevent any build up of materiel able to overwhelm the defences. Even poor quality troops could achieve this from strong fortifications with interlocking fields of fire and nothing in the German experience to date had disproved this. In the blitzkreig operations in 1940, after all, the much vaunted Maginot Line had not been breached, it had been bypassed. Rommel wanted to force the Allies into attacking at a point which would stretch their resources making them even more vulnerable.

Heavy fighting in Russia kept up the pressure on the Germans and the Atlantic Wall defences were afforded second priority, especially after the battle of Kursk when the tide of the war appeared to be turning and the Ost battalions of East European volunteers were viewed with suspicion. These were sent to France to allow more supposedly loyal German troops to be used in their place. The defenders of France were then, in

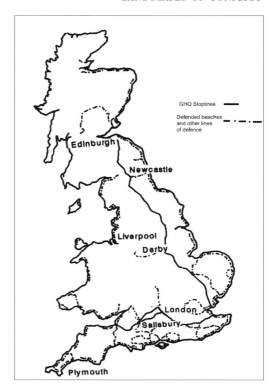

11 With invasion expected at any time, a series of 'stoplines' were put in place around the country to act as lines of defence. Thousands of now forgotten pillboxes and trenches still cover the countryside. Work is still needed to identify how the system would have worked

12 Inside the stopline defences. A contemporary account. *Tim Lynch collection*

13 Atlantic Wall gun emplacement, Normandy

many cases, men who could not speak German, drawn from dozens of ethnic groups across the occupied territories. An extreme example of this is recorded by the historian Stephen Ambrose (1995: 34) who reports the case of Lt Robert Brewer of the US 101st Airborne at Utah Beach, who captured four Koreans. Originally conscripted into the Japanese Army, they had been captured by the Russians in Manchuria before becoming *Wehrmacht* 'volunteers' after their capture on the Eastern Front. Elsewhere, Montgomery wrote of 'Japanese and Turkish' prisoners in British hands. Poorly armed with a variety of German, French and other captured weapons and equipment, the *Wehrmacht* in France had changed little since 1918, with the best men and equipment taken by the elite units of the SS, leaving the army largely reliant on horse power. While the Allies built dummy vehicles to confuse reconnaissance aircraft, the *Wehrmacht* built plaster horses. When Rommel took over tactical responsibility for the defence of France in 1943, he quickly realised the gulf between Hitler's idea of an Atlantic Wall and the reality of the defences in place and began a vigorous programme of building and training to make ready for an invasion that was only a matter of time away.

Along the coastline of Europe, slave labourers and locally drafted builders created a seemingly impenetrable line of fortifications. Giant concrete mixers poured over 600 cubic metres at a time, each square metre reinforced with 60kg of steel. The bunkers were designed to withstand bombardment by means of wide bases sunk into the ground and cushioned with earth to prevent being displaced by near misses. Their embrasures were stepped to allow greater arcs of fire whilst preventing shrapnel from entering. Between the bunkers, small 'Tobruks' provided extra cover for infantrymen. Some even mounted captured tank turrets for extra firepower. To fool Allied planners, bunkers were painted to resemble houses and cafes, had false walls built around them to look like barns or were covered with grass or stone. The beaches before them were strewn with obstacles − steel posts to rip the bottoms of any landing craft, sea and land mines, concrete tank traps and barbed wire. The best and most effective of these fortifications held back the Allied invasion of 6 June 1944 for less time than had been spent pouring the concrete.

Static defences throughout history have suffered the same major drawback − to be effective, the battle has to come to them. By 1944, technological advances, such as the development of specialised armoured vehicles designed to overcome obstacles and the use of airborne troops to land behind the defences, meant that without what military planners refer to as defence in depth, the very rationale for the wall was flawed. Nevertheless, other static defence lines were built and did prove effective in slowing, if not actually stopping, the Allied armies. The end of the Second World War did not see the end of bunker building, but rather an increase, as defences went underground to avoid the threat of nuclear devastation on the surface. Williams (2003) argued that in an age of long range inter-continental missiles carrying conventional or Nuclear, Biological, Chemical (NBC) warheads, the use and design of the stronghold has almost returned to its prehistoric roots. Defences of barbed or razor-wire on top of fencing supported by guard posts are effectively the modern equivalent of a ditch, bank and palisade fence, and despite the growing use of 'smart' bombs released many miles from their targets,

14 German 'Tobruks', Normandy. Note size of the shell crater alongside the Tobruk. Designed for one man, these were linked by trenches to provide quickly accessible strongpoints around the perimeter of larger emplacements to protect against ground attack

local defence is still of some importance. This can be seen as part of a long-established trend in which strongholds have gained increasingly sophisticated defences to counter new weapons systems, only to then revert to seemingly inadequate and outdated ones when the need arises.

> The underlying fact remains that, no matter how ineffective a stronghold's defences might appear to be against the weapons of another age, even those of an earlier time, it was the ability to withstand an attack using contemporary weapons and tactics that was of paramount importance. If an older stronghold could be adapted to resist later weapons, that should be regarded as a bonus. (Williams 2003: 245)

If the defences of the Atlantic Wall were a failure in practice, they were a huge success in propaganda terms. It served a symbolic purpose out of all proportion with its ability to actually dominate the battlefields of Normandy and it is this symbolic purpose that has interested researchers for many years. Architect and social theorist Paul Virilio's seminal work on the Atlantic Wall (1975) opened discussion of a far wider perspective on the nature of conflict and of fortifications than had previously been the norm. Virilio's interest in dromology, the study of speed, led him to consider the use of fortifications in the context of speed, time, technology and representation and their impact on the landscape of twentieth-century warfare (see Gane 1999 for a review of his influence). The nineteenth-century military strategist Karl von Clausewitz considered that the use of force was best directed against the political, economic, and cultural heartland of an enemy. Virilio, though, suggests a modification of Sun Tzu's ancient philosophy that victory is won by using the advantage of perception and seizing the perceptive high ground. It in itself can be seen as echoed in the 'hearts and minds' policy of the US military in Vietnam. If the military can gain the perceptive high ground, then it will receive popular support and thus increase its effectiveness. This policy was rapidly modified by troops on the ground into a more practical strategy described as 'when you have them by the balls, their hearts and minds will follow', but essentially, controlling the attitudes of the population towards the military can be reduced to a simple statement in which it can be argued that it is not necessary to destroy a culture in order to dominate it – Pepsi Cola is as prevalent in Vietnam today as it was in the 1960s because large numbers of people want American domination, albeit a cultural one with the illusion of choice. Construction of huge powerful symbols of military might in this context serve to enforce the perception of control – if the enemy thinks he is beaten, he is. The fall of France in 1940 has been regarded as the inevitable outcome of launching a vastly superior German force against the Allies. In fact, the German Army was outnumbered. Its success, however, owed much to huge symbolic victories that undermined the French government's will to fight rather than its capability. The building of the Atlantic Wall sent a clear message that not only were the Germans victorious, but that they intended to stay. So powerful was this statement that it led to D-Day planners themselves overestimating its potential to halt the landings, even after the failure of the much vaunted Maginot Line to accomplish the same task.

15 The power of any fortification comes as much from its ability to dominate as from any inherent defensive ability. This recreated US firebase of the Vietnam period shows how such structures send a clear message to the local population, if not to a determined enemy

Of all archaeological remains, castles and strongholds are the most obvious, accessible and exciting, since they appear to offer the strongest evidence of conflict as an organised social activity. The emphasis on studying fortification from a purely strategic viewpoint has given way to a much broader recognition that such places serve many functions far beyond their impact on their immediate vicinity. In his essay 'Lessons of the War with Spain, 1899', Alfred Thayer Mahan argued that defensive power does not determine the outcome of war but accepted that some centres need to be protected. For Mahan, fortifications were a cost-effective means of avoiding the need for large standing armies. Coastal fortifications, for example, serve to release naval forces for more offensive use elsewhere. Some years before, in 1843, Lieutenant Halleck, later to become a general in the American Civil War, wrote in respect of US coastal defences that they could 'never exert an influence dangerous to public liberty, but as a means of preserving peace, and as obstacles to an invader, their influence and power are immense' (Lewis 1979: 4). Later, President Grover Cleveland claimed in 1896 that 'we should always keep in mind that of all forms of military preparation coast defence alone is essentially pacific in its nature ... they are not a temptation to war, but security against it' (Lewis 1979: 5).

This perception of the nature and power of coastal defences to protect without threatening demonstrates the symbolic and practical value of all fortifications. Here, they are seen as protecting 'us' from outside invasion. Inland, their function remains the same, but

16 An American firebase controlling the Perfume River, Hue, Vietnam. The river is some distance below the firebase, which is as much a symbol of American might as it is a checkpoint for river traffic

who now are the enemy? If we think of a castle or fort as an aircraft carrier, we can see that it acts as a base for a small effective strike force, able to dominate the area around it without needing the resources taken up by a large fleet. A commander does not need to maintain a large force in order to be able to strike at will into the countryside. The mere presence of the structure itself reinforces that message. In his 1992 article, David Stocker reviewed a number of academic publications on the subject of medieval castles and concluded that most were still in what he termed the 'shadow of the general's armchair', and that studies of castles 'have taken a long time to emerge from the shadow of this approach. The military strategists have long held sway over the social and economic historians' (Stocker 1992: 415). Instead, he suggested new approaches, such as that of Michael Thompson, who, in *Rise of the Castle* wrote that German castle tower placement had an 'essentially symbolic function, "nailing the valley" in which it sits and from which it is supported' (Thompson 1991 in Stocker). At the same time, N.J.G. Pounds' *The Medieval Castle in England and Wales* argued that castle distribution is more a function of legal than military control (1990 in Stocker). It is here that Harrington's (2004) call for more investigation into fortified houses becomes relevant. The use of small, fortified places to symbolise a wider power demonstrates the ability of such places to influence power and control merely by their presence. Who are these places meant for? Do they offer security or threat to people living nearby? Recently, discussion has begun around whether the fortified military and police observation towers

Left, below and opposite: 17-20 Symbolic use of fortifications. The power of strongpoints to dominate the surrounding territory is demonstrated in these examples from France

in Northern Ireland should be preserved as examples of fortification in the same way as would earlier structures for these very reasons. Already, plans are under way to consider what to do with the former high security Maze prison (British Archaeology 84, Sep/Oct 2005) which highlights these very concerns.

We need to study fortifications in the context of the landscape in which they are built. Three broad approaches to the study of landscape have been identified by Brown (1987) which we can adapt to meet this need:

1   An attempt to answer a specific question about the landscape, such as how geographical features affected the course of a particular action or to test a hypothesis about how a campaign may have unfolded

2   A focus on a particular kind of feature (or 'monument' in archaeological terms), such as the siting and development of hill forts within a region or how the anti-invasion defences of 1940 might have interacted

3   A study of the changing uses of military sites over time – for example, a Second World War era gun emplacement still stands, built into the ruins of the Roman fort at Pevensey in East Sussex. How, then, do the anti-invasion defences of the Second World War relate to those of earlier periods?

In particular, his suggestion that the use of sites over time is relevant means that by looking at fortifications within the physical landscape, we can explore such sites with

21 Reusable defences. This Loire chateau bears the scars of fighting in 1944 when German troops held out against the advancing Americans

a view to understanding that there is frequently a continuity in defence, dictated by geography and settlement patterns. Many sites were used and reused, possibly over centuries. The Second World War pillbox, built into the remains of the medieval castle at Pevensey, which itself was built on the remains of a Norman castle and Roman Saxon shore fort, is just one example. At Old Sarum in Wiltshire and Portchester in Hampshire, medieval castles have been constructed within larger Iron Age and Roman defences respectively. Hambledon Hill in Dorset was built to provide defences in the Neolithic period but served the same function during the Iron Age and, over a millennium later, for the 'Clubmen' in the Civil War during 1645. The nineteenth-century fortifications at Tilbury were built over a Henrican fort. The effectiveness of these older fortifications in resisting later and more sophisticated means of attack, for which they were not designed, raises questions about those histories of castles and defences which concentrate primarily on the military and technical aspects of their design for the period in which they were originally constructed (Planel 1995: 5).

Given that the greatest distribution of fortification sites is along the boundaries of territory, it is not hard to accept that their function is as much symbolic as practical. Again following Brown, we can also begin to look at specific types of monument within the landscape and at what it can tell us about the differing types of conflict and warfare at the time. Defensive structures have been a feature of warfare throughout history. James Dyer (2003) writes that evidence shows that hilltops in the UK were being fortified over 5000 years ago with a peak of building between the sixth and fourth centuries BC. Study shows that such structures were used to defend against cattle raids as much as full-scale invasion and we need to identify them in terms of the type of conflict they responded to – military, social, economic, tribal or national. Mainly to be found west of a line between the Mersey and the Solent, Dyer reports that the 1962 Ordnance Survey 'Map of Southern Britain in the Iron Age' included some 1366 sites directly related to defensive structures across these southern areas of the country, but adds that they are also to be found further north, albeit in smaller numbers, and he identifies five main types to be found:

1	Contour Forts	These he describes as 'classic' hill forts where a line of defences follows the natural contours of the ground
2	Promontory Forts	These rely on natural features, such as coastal headlands where an earthwork across the feature can form an effective barrier to attackers
3	Plateau Forts	Sited on flat ground and reliant entirely on man-made defence works
4	Valley Forts	Rare sub-type of plateau forts which need to be heavily defended since obviously an enemy would have the advantage of high ground
5	Multiple enclosure or Hillslope Forts	Apparently confined to the south and west, these are sited on the slope of a hill and often overlooked by high ground

Given the difficulties in defending some of these sites, it has been suggested that they may not in fact be 'forts' as we would understand them any more perhaps than many 'castles' built over the past few centuries. There was a tendency to create pseudo-military defences for decorative purposes from the late Tudor period onward and many country homes were designed to act as displays of power and wealth rather than as effective fortifications against attack. However, Hill and Wileman have suggested that these differences in siting of 'forts' in seemingly inappropriate places and their style of construction can be seen as reflecting an ever evolving and increasingly sophisticated understanding of the use of tactics. The location and construction of forts, they suggest, owes more to proximity to the thing to be protected – an important river crossing or road junction, religious site, economic centre or other site – than to a consideration of 'natural defensibility'. It is here that conflict arises between the study of forts as military centres as opposed to their function as political foci. However, in a great many cases, an analysis of their common features and the archaeological and historical evidence from their investigation shows that, not only were there some extremely sophisticated military design features incorporated into their structures, but also that actual evidence of attack could be found. Those forts in positions which may be regarded as poor choices for a defensive structure, for instance, could be designed to force attackers to approach the entrance with their right, unshielded sides exposed to the defenders on the ramparts and thus provide a highly effective barrier. The Belgae developed a system of hedges planted with thorn and briar that proved capable of breaking up Roman cavalry movements and infantry attack, and similar defences were brought into Britain. Complex patterns of dykes and mounds may not provide long-term protection from a determined assault but they could serve to disrupt the attackers long enough for the defenders to inflict heavy casualties before escaping. Caesar's forces in Britain are known to have fought to overcome such barriers, only to find the inhabitants gone when they finally breached the walls. As the Romans attempted to negotiate their way through such confusing earthworks, lightly armed Britons were able to strike and retreat into cover at minimal risk (Wileman and Hill 2002: 68).

Hillforts gradually gave way to Roman fortifications and later to Anglo-Saxon 'burghs'. Later still came the Norman motte and bailey forts, and finally their stone built castles. At each stage, we see an arms race under way as builders create ever more complex designs to maximise their potential as defensive structures. During the seventeenth century, the Frenchman Sebastien Vauban brought the art of fortification to its peak when he created thirty-three new frontier fortifications and rebuilt a further 300, each making full use of the firepower available to it and incorporating ideas and designs that would still be in use centuries later. In the 1860s, 'Palmerston's Follies', a series of never completed coastal defences along the south coast, sprang from yet another threat of invasion. Almost a century later, thousands of pillboxes appeared within a few short months of war, to be followed over the next four decades by Cold War bunkers in an almost unbroken history of development and redevelopment of the symbols of security. Space here does not allow for a detailed examination of the development of such places but there are already a number of excellent works available detailing the many types of

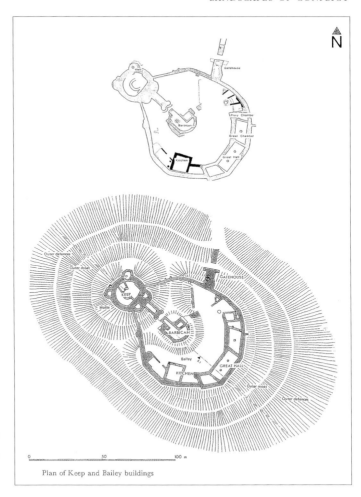

22 Site plan, Sandal Castle, Wakefield. Note the use of hatchards to indicate slopes and earthworks. *From Butler, 1991*

monuments still in existence (See for example Hogg (1975), Friar (2003) or Williams (2003) for more detailed discussions of the evolution of fortifications in general, Dyer (2003) for the development of hillforts, the Council for British Archaeology (2002) and Osborne (2004) for twentieth century structures).

Within the context of this book, each of the thousands of existing fortified sites offers scope for investigation. The Defence of Britain Project (2002), for example, showed the value of volunteer support in order to document the huge number of sites from one period alone. Across the country, other sites await further exploration and studies, such as that undertaken by Hegarty, Newsome and Winton (2005) of Suffolk's anti-invasion defences, can provide valuable information even if, as they point out, the Suffolk coast was not a battlefield in the traditional sense. There can be no doubt that despite this, it was directly involved in an important stage of the Second World War and an important part of Britain's wider coastal anti-invasion landscape – what they argue could be called a 'potential battlefield'. No site or structure of this potential battlefield constitutes a 'place of conflict' as such, but viewed as a whole, the defences of the Suffolk coast were 'as much a "landscape of conflict" as a landscape of defence, the surviving features the remains of possibly the greatest battlefield that never was' (2005: 71).

Appendix A highlights the approaches currently being undertaken in the field of the study of fortifications in one region and these include a number of direct links to issues already highlighted here. For now, perhaps the final word on these landscapes of defence should go to Geoffrey Williams, who reminds us that there are thousands of examples of fortification across Britain, ranging from tiny Neolithic camps to the mighty medieval castles and the all-encompassing defences of Stronghold Britain in the Second World War. Each site has its story to tell but it is important to remember that they do not exist in isolation. They need to be understood as part of a much wider landscape. Williams writes:

> Even more important, whether they be derelict, restored, a museum or converted to another use, remember that all strongholds were working environments devised for a specific purpose. They were built, lived in and manned by real people; few British readers will not have relatives who were involved with a stronghold of some sort in the twentieth century. One must envisage and recreate strongholds in the mind's eye as living places, not as the cold and empty ruins they now often appear (2003: 245-6).

LANDSCAPES OF OFFENCE

It goes without saying that defensive structures guard against attack. As we have already seen, a millennia-long arms race has developed between the need to defend and a need to overcome defences. But whilst the need to defend remains relatively constant, the actual threat fluctuates over time. Landscapes of offence are therefore constructed, not from an intent to remain static, but for the sole purpose of overcoming the enemy. As a result, for much of history, the evidence of the attack has disappeared and it is only where the two landscapes collide, in siegeworks, that any evidence remains. The great strongpoints of Britain often bear the scars of attack, but whilst their walls still stand, the areas around them have frequently been redeveloped. We can see where attackers fired their muskets and cannonballs at the walls, but we rarely find the evidence of where the defenders were aiming. In the context of the English Civil War, Peter Harrington argues that evidence for offensive operations, such as siegeworks, for attacking a place, defensive earthworks to protect the attackers from any potential threat to the rear, the adaptation of adjacent buildings and structures, including barns and churches, and the re-use of earlier earthworks, such as medieval moats, as places from which to conduct offensive operations are all temporary in nature and thus less likely to survive over time, as are the temporary cemeteries for the casualties incurred during attacks (Harrington 2004: 78-9). Few of these features were constructed as long-term projects and so, although they are to be found, they are comparatively rare.

By the age of Vauban in the late seventeenth and early eighteenth centuries, the bastioned fortress was perhaps the most important feature in European warfare. During sieges, 'saps' or trenches would be dug progressively closer to enemy strongholds – hence 'sapper', a term for a military engineer. This would allow infantry to avoid a dash across defended open ground in an assault. Mortars and grenades made an ever increasing contribution to the battlefield during this period. Wellington's Penninsula campaign was marked by a series of bloody assaults on defended towns following sieges – Badajoz would cost the British 3000 casualties alone – but again, evidence of these works would rapidly disappear after use.

Some offensive structures are known to exist, others may exist without being recognised for what they are. For the most part, though, evidence of offensive behaviour away from fixed defences can only become apparent through the systematic and painstaking analysis of archaeological finds and especially through the charting of concentrations of weapons finds. Research into the mapping of deposits of English Civil War bullets, for example, has helped locate troop deployments on the field of Edgehill and Naseby that completely overturn the accepted historical accounts (see Foard 2001, 2004, 2005). Similar work in the United States on the Little Big Horn battlefield has taken this still further, using forensics to chart the movements of individual weapons through the course of the battle (Wason 2003: 198-203; Scott 1989).

At the battle of Waterloo in 1815, British soldiers were mainly armed with the India Pattern musket – purchased in large quantities from the East India Company. With minor modifications, the 'brown bess' had been in service for around eighty years. Fired in volley into massed ranks of enemy troops at ranges of less than 50m, it was a devastating weapon. However, like most weapons of the day, it was not accurate. Colonel Hanger, writing the year before Waterloo, had commented that a musket ball fired by the brown bess could hit a man-sized target at 80yds (around 70m) – but that a soldier would be 'very unfortunate indeed (to) be wounded by a common musket at 150yds (125m) provided his antagonist aims at him; and as to firing at a man at 200 … You may as well fire at the moon' (quoted in Adkin 2001: 166). Hanger was referring to tests on the ranges in Britain. In action, Adkin (p.165) records that the chances of hitting an individual with an aimed shot at 100m were around one in thirty. At 50-70m, this improved to one in three. Combat, by necessity, relied on disciplined, well-trained troops standing their ground until the enemy approached to a range at which the weapons would become effective and then it became simply a question of who could maintain the greater rate of fire. The evidence is thus concentrated into a narrow area where lines of infantrymen can be traced through the numbers of balls to be found in the topsoil.

Fifty years later, during the American Civil War, it was estimated that men armed with muskets like these used 240lbs of powder and 900lbs of lead for every man actually hit. These antiquated firearms were pitted against the latest British made Enfield muskets, capable of penetrating 3.25in (8.25cm) of seasoned pine wood at ranges of over 1000yds (900m). At just 200yds (183m), a range at which the brown bess might have been used to fire at the moon, it could penetrate 11in (28cm) of wood. Tests of the Springfield rifle in 1861 showed that a man was capable of firing ten times in five minutes, and at 100yds (90m) could put all ten into a target less than 1ft (31cm) square. At ranges of up to 500yds (460m), he could hit a target 4ft (120cm) square (William C. Davis, *Fighting Men of the Civil War*, Undated, p.52). This rapid advance in firepower technology overtook many longer serving officers, notably Union General John Sedgewick, who, on 9 May 1864 at Spotsylvania, is said to have been hit in the head as he uttered the immortal phrase 'they couldn't hit an elephant at this dist …' Although unfortunately, as with all great war stories, it's not entirely true. Major-General Martin McMahon was with him on that fateful day:

> About an hour before, I had remarked to the general, pointing to the two pieces in a half-jesting manner, which he well understood, 'General, do you see that section of artillery? Well, you are not to go near it today.' He answered good-naturedly, 'McMahon, I would like to know who commands this corps, you or I?' I said, playfully, 'Sometimes I am in doubt myself'; but added, 'Seriously, General, I beg of you not to go to that angle; every officer who has shown himself there has been hit, both yesterday and to-day'.

Sedgewick replied that he saw no reason to go there anyway. As the two men began to deploy their troops, bullets whistled by and some of the men dodged. The general joked with them about being afraid of sporadic shots and asking what they would do when they were faced with volley fire, adding that they 'couldn't hit an elephant at that distance'. A few seconds later, a man who had been separated from his regiment passed directly in front of the general and, at the same moment, a sharp-shooter's bullet cracked past so that the soldier, who was then just in front of the general, dodged to the ground. The general touched him gently with his foot and again joked about dodging random fire, repeating his remark. The man rose, saluted and said good-naturedly, 'General, I dodged a shell once, and if I hadn't, it would have taken my head off. I believe in dodging.' The general laughed and sent the man to his place. McMahon then recalled that a third shot rang out and 'the general's face turned slowly to me, the blood spurting from his left cheek under the eye in a steady stream. He fell in my direction; I was so close to him that my effort to support him failed, and I fell with him' (in Johnson, R.U. and Buell, C., *Battles and Leaders of the Civil War* New York 1887-8). McMahon's account, though, includes a telling phrase: 'every officer who has shown himself there has been hit'. Individuals, not formations, had become targets of ever-improving weapons technology.

The American Civil War was a turning point between the old style of blunt instrument warfare conducted up close and personal and the new, industrial mass destruction that would spread to ranges unimaginable to those who had fought at Waterloo. With it came a recognition that the days of standing still to deliver steady volleys into an enemy who conveniently marched within range were long gone. Even at the beginning of the war, the academy at West Point was teaching its officer cadets that engineering and the spade were now full partners in war with the infantry, cavalry and artillery. The Confederate General Lee, now better remembered as a field commander, was nicknamed 'the ace of spades' by his men for the amount of digging he ordered them to do in the first year of the war. In many campaigns over the following years, trenches and rifle scrapes found their way with ever greater frequency into field actions. Where time allowed, simple

23 As troops sought cover from ever more accurate rifle fire, trenches became a common feature of the battlefield, here as a frontline fire trench and as a communication line to the rear areas

holes in the ground were supplemented by logs and by carefully cleared fields of fire in front of them. It has been suggested that earthworks of varying kinds were particularly popular in the Civil War, not only because rifles and artillery were improving in range and accuracy and therefore the need to find shelter had increased, but more significantly because the existence of strong points had a steadying effect upon armies which were predominantly made up of conscripted citizen soldiers (Bull 2003: 7). It was a recognition not confined to America. Across the world, armies were forced to look to the spade as an essential infantry tool. Gone were the days of a unit marching into the attack as a mass. Gradually, they were beginning to spread out in order to reduce casualties. They were also spending far longer in range of the defenders' guns, making attacks longer than anyone had previously known. Defenders could expect to have the advantage of cover but in the attack, infantry needed to find cover from accurate rifle and artillery fire if enough of them were to reach their objective to be effective (Bull 2003 reports that, at the time, an estimated five attackers for every defender was considered to be the minimum required for a successful assault). Where natural cover could not be found, temporary 'rifle scrapes' – a shallow trench just big enough for a rifleman to lie prone without exposing himself to return fire – would be needed.

Elsewhere, the British colonial experience, especially on India's North–West Frontier, had shown how accurate fire had achieved one of the military's overarching objectives – economy of force. Entire regiments could be held up and badly mauled by relatively few good marksmen firing from 'sangars'. These were firing positions in rocky terrain, sometimes supplemented by the addition of further rocks to fill any gaps in the natural cover. The word entered British military parlance and has stayed there to this day to refer to any small prepared position. The fighting against Boer commandoes in South Africa further demonstrated the need to create some form of cover for an attacking force against mobile and deadly accurate snipers. By 1914, the use of trenches was already an established fact of warfare but already military authorities were becoming concerned that defensive works could undermine the aggression needed to take the battle to the enemy. The British Army manual *Infantry Training 1914* stressed the need for all soldiers to be aware of 'the general principles of the siting of trenches, the construction of overhead cover, and the circumstances in which trenches are required' (HMSO 1914: 12). These circumstances, however, were specific. Field fortifications were defined as:

> … those measures which may be taken for the defence of positions intended to be only temporarily held. Works of this kind are executed either in the face of the enemy or in anticipation of his immediate approach … field fortification presupposes a defensive attitude and, though recourse to it may under certain circumstances be desirable, IT MUST ALWAYS BE REGARDED AS A MEANS TO AN END, AND NOT AN END IN ITSELF (Manual of Field Engineering 1911. HMSO cited in Bull 2003: 25).

The official manuals were themselves supplemented by private publications, such as E.J. Solano's 1914 *Field Entrenchments: Spadework for Riflemen* and Edmund Dane's 1915 *Trench Warfare*, offering practical advice for men at the front on the amount of earth required

24 A communication line to the rear areas

25 Where
entrenchment
was not possible,
'sangars' built
above the ground
provided cover

to stop a rifle bullet (roughly the same as the length of a rifle) and how to improvise protective cover (Bull 2003). Within days of the declaration of war, British infantry were digging 'lying trenches', an oblong 6ft long by 2ft wide with a small bank of earth facing the enemy to act as cover and as a rifle rest (Holmes 2004: 246), but doctrine dictated that these were only ever intended to be a means by which to consolidate ground taken and to provide a jumping-off point for assaults. It was a doctrine, as we have seen, that would remain in force throughout the next four years and would profoundly influence the design and development of Allied entrenchments in marked contrast to those of the enemy.

By the outbreak of the Second World War, tactics had developed into a more mobile form of warfare, in which soldiers facing artillery, tanks and aerial bombardment needed to spread out across the battlefield in order to reduce casualties and defend far greater tracts of terrain than had previous generations. Slit trenches or 'foxholes' became the norm, affecting not only the deployment of troops but their effectiveness too. In a post war study of US troops' performance during 1943-5, Colonel S.L.A. Marshall found that as few as 15 per cent of men on the front lines would actually use their weapons, even

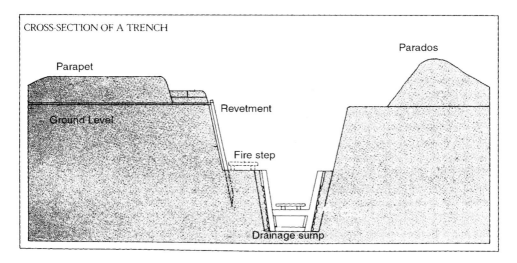

CROSS-SECTION OF A TRENCH

Parados

Parapet

Ground Level

Revetment

Fire step

Drainage sump

26 Cross section of a fire trench

under attack. In earlier wars, men had fought shoulder to shoulder with their comrades and were drilled to simply perform routine functions of loading, firing and manœuvring as a mass. Now individual soldiers spread widely across the battlefield had to make individual decisions that would cost the life of other human beings and few could face doing so. The exception to this was being on the so-called 'crew-served weapons, such as machine guns, bazookas and mortars, where two or more men were needed and where they would have witnesses to their failure. Even in the most aggressive units, Marshall claimed, the figure rarely rose above 25 per cent of troops, no matter how long the action took (Marshall 1947: 56-7). For the first time in history, soldiers' experience of war had become an isolated one in which most riflemen were out of sight of each other and therefore the decision to actively take part and to kill had become an individual, not a group, choice. Soldiers are not remote from the social, moral and political landscape of the culture that spawned them. In war, they are 'our boys' in a very real sense. They are what their society has made them. If society chooses to glorify those who have made the 'great sacrifice', the more pragmatic acknowledge that wars are not won by dying for one's country but by making the other man die for his. In the years since 1945, soldiers have become even more divorced from their primary function to close with and defeat the enemy by the ongoing race to develop new and ever-more effective methods of achieving this. Despite this, in an age of laser guided weaponry and 'smart' bombs, it is still left to the infantryman with rifle and bayonet to take and control ground in much the same way as he has throughout recorded history. Understanding the landscape of offence is therefore about combining an appreciation of the overall need of the commanders to deliver an effective use of force against a selected target by ensuring that as many troops as possible survive the initial 'advance to contact' and actually reach their goal with an understanding of the group dynamics in operation to motivate the individual to maintain the attack, even when separated from his or her peers.

27 English Civil War pikemen on the march. This is probably how Newcastle's men would have appeared at the time of the Tankersley battle. See p.79

UNDERSTANDING THE EVIDENCE

So what role does the battlefield archaeologist play in developing this understanding? We have already seen that there is a need to deepen our understanding, not only of the practical development of defensive structures, especially those of the twentieth century, but also by examining their interrelation within the physical landscape. Such work is ongoing (e.g. Lacey 2003; Foot 2003, 2004; Osborne 2004) but more is needed on, for example, which sites were positioned primarily as a visual symbol of defence to bolster civilian morale. A number of loopholes cut into house walls for home defence have been identified by the Defence of Britain survey. How effective could these have been against panzers? Yet they demonstrated to a frightened population that something was being done to protect them. Such a study offers a multilayered understanding, not only about military determinants over time, but also the increasingly important anthropological role such places have in creating the climate or landscape in which actions take place.

Defence works are the most tangible, and therefore most studied, aspect of this approach. They are fixed and (usually) easy to locate in both time and space. By contrast, offensive landscapes, by their very nature, are generally more widespread, transient and therefore ethereal. Nevertheless, evidence is there to be found. This evidence offers a chance to develop an understanding of the use of tactics by attackers and how they perceived the same landscape. The avenue of approach needs to be identified to understand where the threats were assumed to be. The start line must be found to understand how the attackers would have formed for the final assault and finally, evidence of the route of the attack traced through the material evidence located in the topsoil. In one case, a returning Falklands veteran joined an official military tour of the battlefield on which he fought. Having been led up a slope by the guide, the veteran politely redirected the tour to a spot about 200m away, where a trail of cartridge cases led up the hill (Islander Pat Whitney, personal communication 2002). The story demonstrates that assaults are rarely textbook examples. Weather conditions, supplies, enemy positions and many other factors can affect what actually happens and we need to be careful about superimposing later assumptions onto actual events. We need, as we shall see, to view the ground, not from the perspective of the tourist today, but from that of the soldier on the day.

In a later chapter we will look at identifying monuments in the physical landscape, including those characteristic of offensive operations. For now, what is important is to recognise that battles represent merely a snapshot in time, in which military action took place on a certain site. At the same time, we need to balance the often competing needs of those with an interest in studying conflict and those responsible for managing the landscape. Battlefields are more than just the arena in which battles take place. They are part of a much wider social and economic landscape and have been, and will continue to be, managed with this in mind. We cannot expect a battlefield to be maintained in pristine condition as it was on the day. What we need to do is to recover and record as much information about it as is possible before the combined forces of nature and man destroy the evidence. In the case of twentieth-century conflict, we need to do this whilst there is still time to incorporate the direct oral evidence of those who can tell us most. For many, the recent past is not yet history, let alone archaeology – but one day it will be.

2

RESEARCH DESIGN

Research designs, or 'explications' as they are sometimes known, set out to detail what will be done, how, why and to what end. It seems obvious that before embarking on any project, it is useful to have some plan. So obvious, in fact, that it was not until the development of what is known as 'processual archaeology' (the study of the process of adaptation of cultures over time) in the 1960s that detailed research designs began to appear following recommendations contained in a paper by Lewis Binford in 1964. The move towards this more scientific approach was not always welcomed in British archaeology but 'the shift that research designs typified was to dig in order to answer questions rather than to dig for things' (Gamble 2004: 48) and today they are not only accepted but have become a standard requirement of any piece of archaeological work. A good research design will not inevitably lead to good research, but at least it will highlight the questions that need to be asked and provide structure to the project. The development of a research design is especially important for the amateur researcher who needs to fit their study around the demands of work, family and budget constraints. It will minimise wasted time and effort if it is properly prepared. Rudyard Kipling defined the necessary facts to be determined when he wrote of his 'six serving men' – the answers to the questions of who, what, where, why, when and how.

The next chapter discusses the factors that will influence what information is sought and selected, and so a research design is about recognising that these factors will inevitably have impacted on source material. It helps us to begin to structure questions appropriately and to determine what the research is intended to do – is it a search for evidence to support the existing version of events or an attempt to re-interpret them? Is it about debunking myths or about understanding how and why those myths developed? Once these theoretical frameworks are understood, we are in a position to consider the practical steps needed to design a framework for research.

STEP ONE

Kipling's 'honest serving men' are perhaps the best starting point for any planned piece of research. Begin by asking yourself:

1 What?	What do I want to do? Do you want to write a book or just satisfy your own curiosity? Do you want to complete a piece of desk-based research or actually work on-site?
2 Why?	Why do I want to do it? What is it that interests you about this and will keep you motivated once you start?
3 When?	When do you have time to undertake the work and complete it? Is this something you can only do at weekends (when archives are likely to be closed)? Will you be able to devote the time you need to it?
4 How?	How do I start? What do you need before you set out?
5 Where?	Where do I start? What do you already know about it? What do you need to know next?
6 Who?	Who can help me? What resources are open to you? Local historians, authors, re-enactors, veterans and museum staff may all be able to offer pieces of the jigsaw. Is there anyone else who can help with the work or might be interested in just coming along to see what you're doing?

All these questions are about developing what the business world calls SMART objectives. These are:

1 Specific:	The simpler the project, the greater its chances of success
2 Measurable:	You need to be able to see that progress is being made
3 Achievable:	You need to be able to finish what you have started and keep it within your abilities. There must be something for you to work with
4 Realistic:	It must be something that you are able to accomplish realistically. Setting out to study a battlesite a long way from home if you have a limited income to fund travel costs is not realistic
5 Time limited:	You (and your family) need to know that there will be an end to it all and that this will be marked by something – a book, a visit or even just an announcement that you've finished

STEP TWO

Having established what your project will involve, the next step is to decide on what questions you are trying to answer. In the previous chapter, Brown's (1987) approaches to landscape were adapted to meet the needs of military landscape analysis but within the scope of this book, we can also add a more intimate approach by looking at the landscape of war as it would have been experienced by the individual – what would your ancestor have seen when he or she stood here?

Again, Kipling's questions are useful to focus thinking onto specific issues.

1 What?	What do you want to know? What is already known? What questions do you want to ask about your subject? What factors may be relevant?
2 Why?	Why are these relevant? How do they increase what you already know and how will they help you?
3 When?	What period(s) are you interested in and how do they relate to your subject? What dating evidence is available to you?
4 How?	How was your target involved in the events you are studying?
5 Where?	Where is your target and how does it relate to others nearby? If it is a pillbox, where are the others? Where is it defending and why?
6 Who?	Who fought here? Who built it? Who might be able to tell you more about it?

STEP THREE

Putting all this together in a short document will not only serve to clarify the aims and outcomes of your project, but will also help to prevent your research wandering off on a tangent when some interesting, but unconnected, information comes to light. A SMART project will be completed, but a ramble through local history, however enjoyable, will ultimately lead nowhere.

STEP FOUR

The process of research should be one of continual review and re-assessment of progress, using these same questions to act as quality control. Each fact needs to be weighed against the same criteria so that its value can be measured and new theories developed and tested. Once a research design is in place, the real research can begin. In the following chapters we will explore the process of desk-top assessments and how these relate to fieldwork.

3

SOURCES: FINDING AND USING DOCUMENTS

Half a century ago, A.H. Burne, one of the earliest battlefield historians, explained in his seminal book *The Battlefields of England* that his motive was one of trying to help people find for themselves some of the pivotal sites in British history. He wrote with dismay at the barriers facing anyone attempting to find reliable information from guidebooks or local residents. General histories, he pointed out, are often brief and too wide ranging to provide any useful detail about specific locations. Local histories are more likely to include legends handed down over generations than an objective account of events and are rarely produced by military historians. Burne wrote:

> To give but one example, the field of Naseby is in the heart of the country; there are but two human habitations in the vicinity. I recently visited both of them. At one I learnt – nothing; at the other I was pointed out an oak-tree up which Cromwell, or it might have been Prince Rupert hid – my informant was not certain on the point.

In the years since Burne began his work, the past has become big business. Presenting our heritage has developed into a national industry and, at first glance, a visit to the 'Military History' or 'Local Interest' section of any large bookshop would suggest there is a huge amount of information available that Burne might have envied. Unfortunately, as Burne points out, even where a battle is well known, our knowledge of it often comes from the information handed down to us without ever considering the most obvious problem when dealing with the past – human error. On 6 June 1944, a force of US Rangers undertook a crucial action at the *Pointe-du-Hoc* in Normandy, an action frequently referred to, especially in American accounts, as the *Pointe-du-Hoe*. Any English traveller who regularly visits France is likely to be bemused by the apparent French inability to pronounce their language properly, or even to recognise it no matter how loudly it is shouted at them, but even the most ardent Francophobe must accept that they are able to spell their own place names. In fact, the problem lies in a simple typographical error by D-Day planners that has since gone into the history books.

More recently, on 8 June 1982, during the war in the South Atlantic, Argentine A4B Skyhawk fighter–bombers of V *Brigada Aera* attacked two British landing ships, the

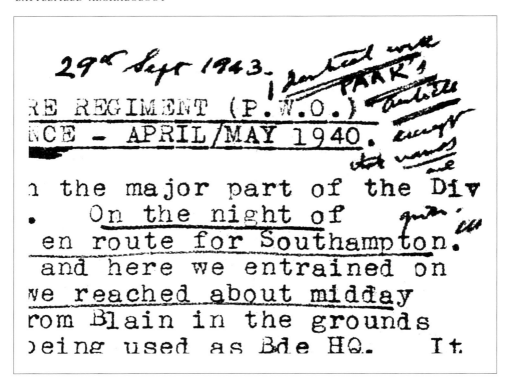

28 Handwriting can often be indecipherable, even if in a modern script! *Tim Lynch collection*

Sir Galahad and *Sir Tristram*, as they lay at anchor, killing more than fifty soldiers and sailors, and wounding many more. On shore nearby were journalists and film crews accompanying the Task Force who later reported the incident back to the UK. The disaster at Bluff Cove became one of the most controversial and infamous episodes of the Falklands War, but journalism, it has been said, is history in a hurry.

Twenty-five years later, visitors to Bluff Cove on the Falkland Islands are redirected to nearby Pleasant Bay, just south of the settlement of Fitzroy. This is where the attack actually took place. Years after the event, a veteran was approached by a television company asking about his experiences. He had been at Fitzroy on that fateful day, close enough to feel the concussion of the bombs and heat of the fires they triggered. The researcher listened politely to his story and then asked if he knew of anybody who had been at Bluff Cove and seen the bombings there. Others have reported amateur historians seizing on the fact that they had 'got it wrong' in recounting their experiences. In an age of satellite communications, where journalists act as professional witnesses to history, a major incident was comprehensively misplaced within hours of it happening. What chance, then, for a battle fought hundreds of years ago?

This chapter is about gathering the right type of information to understand events on a battlefield. It will look at the sources, and how to use them, and it will provide examples of research methodology. Any attempt to trace an action will inevitably start with desk-based research using both primary (first hand accounts, records and reports) and secondary (later versions) sources. Both are invaluable. Both need to be treated with care.

SECONDARY SOURCES

The starting point for any investigation into military history is likely to be through what are termed as 'secondary sources'. These are the accounts produced after the event by people who were not there at the time and have been produced with the benefit of hindsight. As we have seen in the previous chapter, these accounts can become assimilated into popular culture, until, in some cases, they achieve an almost legendary status. Often, this status is deliberately fostered and before starting to gather the evidence together, it is important to understand how these processes affect the information available.

In approaching secondary information, we need to be aware of what communication theorists refer to as 'gatekeeping' by the author. Information is edited to fit with a certain argument or point of view. This may be simply human error, as in accounts of the *Pointe-du-Hoe* and Bluff Cove, a failure to check the origins of stories (see Hayward 2002, 2003, for examples from the First and Second World Wars), a desire to honour the participants that overtakes objectivity (a criticism sometimes leveled at American historian Stephen Ambrose for his series of the Second World War accounts of US servicemen) or a more overt, even sinister, political agenda (such as Holocaust denial). It is vital, then, to attempt to identify the author's sources and intent before accepting their analysis.

Designing an effective piece of research requires an ability to assess the quality of the information currently available and that in itself requires an understanding of what has been recorded, why that information has been recorded over perhaps other accounts, when it was recorded – at the time, in the immediate aftermath or many years later, how something has been recorded and remembered – as first-hand testimony, hearsay evidence from a third party or as a propaganda tool, where it was recorded – in official reports, in personal memoirs, in diaries or in some other form of record, and finally who our sources are – are they perhaps someone with a need to prolong a particular version of history? We'll never really know how many celebrated feats of great tactical thinking and leadership were actually the results of commanders getting lost on their way to the fight because, history, after all, is written by the winning side and few ambitious officers are likely to admit that they just got lucky. As Winston Churchill is said to have put it, 'history will bear me out, particularly as I shall write that history myself'. We need to bear that in mind when starting any historical investigation, and particularly so with military history where a great many people have a vested interest in the 'right' story being told. It is vital that, in sitting down to plan a systematic study of an event, we are aware of where our own prejudices, theories and beliefs about the event come from, so that we can build in measures to ensure that we do not overlook significant facts simply because they do not fit into our version of the story so that we choose not to find them.

Whether we use primary or secondary sources as our starting point, we need to remember that these have been written from one perspective. Sometimes this perspective can overtake the reality and, in the public mind at least, become the 'true' story. Hayward (2003, 2004) ably demonstrates how myths and legends of the First and Second World Wars have found their way into mainstream historiography, and Clarke (2004) takes this further in his study of the use of stories of supernatural support for the British troops and Mons and elsewhere. The 'spin' put onto the blunders which led to the costly and doomed 'Charge of the Light Brigade' by the Victorian establishment is a further example of how the story can be valued more highly than the history. 'Honour the Light Brigade' demanded Tennyson's stirring account of the ill-fated charge. Yet as Victorian children learned the poem by heart, and thrilled to the image of true British heroes winning neverending glory, wounded survivors of the Light Brigade were being abandoned to the workhouse (see for example Brighton 2004).

The fact is, as we have already seen, most of what we know about history is a myth – not a lie, but a construct created by the political climate of the times which leads to the development of certain patterns of belief in order to enable us as a society to make some kind of sense of the world around us. The mythology of non-industrial societies, says anthropologist Claude Levi-Strauss, should, in fact, be read as a guide to appropriate behaviour for a given society. These myths form the basis for an understanding of how a society wishes to be seen – hence the British myths surrounding the Blitz of the Second World War is one of how civilians bravely banded together in the face of a common enemy. In this mythology, defiant British people stood up to the worst that Nazi tyranny could throw at them and emerged triumphant. The ordinary Londoner sat through the nightly bombing raids, listening to big bands on the radio or having a 'knees-up' in the underground stations before emerging to carry on as normal. It was the epitome of a proud, brave and resilient people who refused to be cowed by attacks on their homes.

There is, of course, a great deal of truth in that picture. But if we analyse it rationally, we can see problems. If the British people were not bowed by air attack, why then did the RAF sustain such losses to do the same thing to the enemy? Did ordinary Londoners tough it out or was there, quite simply, nowhere else for them to go? Accounts tell of the co-operation and comradeship of the Blitz, but other accounts also survive of rescue workers being hampered in their attempts to recover the wounded and dying from the rubble by looters stealing valuables from the same casualties. Crime rates soared as the sirens acted as signals to burglars, telling them when homes would be empty and when the occupiers would begin to emerge from the shelters.

DECONSTRUCTING HISTORY

Before embarking on a study of history, we need first to understand where it comes from. To do that, we need to deconstruct what we know about an event or people to explore what alternative theories might exist about the reasons why things happened as they did.

In Britain, we can look at the stories of Robin Hood as an example of how deconstruction can offer new perspectives on a subject. In the stories, Robin is a nobleman, wrongfully deprived of his lands by a corrupt usurper to the throne. He takes to the woods, gathers around him a loyal band of fellow outlaw rebels and fights a guerrilla war until the true king returns and all is returned to normal.

In countless books, stories, films, plays and even cartoons, Robin is put forward as epitomising the essence of an English gentleman – defender of the weak, saviour of the poor, loyal to his king. Now let's look at the story more objectively. Robin, famously, steals from the rich to give to the poor – a far more cost-effective use of his time than stealing from the poor, who, by definition, have nothing much for him to steal. A cost-benefit analysis will quickly show that stealing from the rich is a fairly obvious way for an outlaw to support himself. Once he has stolen, he shares the booty with the local peasants. Is this out of concern for their wellbeing or because, like all guerrilla leaders, he knows that the support of the local population is vital? He needs to be able to trade with them since, as an outlaw hiding out in the forest, he's not in a position to produce his own food or pop down to the shops when the fancy takes him. At the same time, given that there is a reward out for him, he knows that if he does not pay them off they'll probably turn him in. Although Robin fights the injustice of a corrupt government, at no point is the king's absolute right to rule questioned, nor does he hesitate to accept his estates back and presumably to fund these by taxing the same peasants he so recently claimed to serve. The story is about ensuring that the status quo is maintained by laying out the behaviour we expect from our heroes. Myths develop within the political framework of their times. The legends of King Arthur and his chivalrous knights, and of Robin Hood, for example, grew in popularity in Victorian times, when the importance of believing that Englishmen represented the most noble and chivalrous breed of humanity and thus had an obligation to help others to achieve the same high standards was central to an underlying imperialist ideology.

In 1984, George Orwell observed that 'whoever controls the present controls the past. Who controls the past controls the future'. History, archaeology and politics are inextricably linked. The political climate in which research has taken place has for many years determined what should be studied and how. Bruce Trigger (1989) argues that three significant contexts can be identified in this respect, each with its own mythology and implications for archaeology:

Nationalist

An anthropological anecdote tells of a Victorian Englishman on safari in Africa. One day, he encounters an African being attacked by a lion and shoots the lion. The next day he sees the same African fighting a white man. He shoots the African. Later, he comes across two white men. One is the man he saved earlier whom he now knows to be French, the other, a man he knows from school in England. He shoots the Frenchman.

The story could go on with ever-finer distinctions. The point is that we all divide the world into three main groups – 'us', 'people like us' and 'others'. We define ourselves by reference to these groups. Across Europe, even today, nations are not firmly established.

Ethnic conflict is rife and with that comes the need to prove the legitimacy of each side's claim to territory. The archaeological and historical evidence of settlement over time becomes a propaganda weapon to support the development of a national identity.

The nationalist movements within the UK have banded together in their respective countries to protest against the destruction of their cultures by the English. However, this overlooks the question of whether a 'nation' existed prior to the English takeover. The question 'when was "Wales"?' has been put forward as part of this discussion. Just as Scotland and Ireland were not separate nations, but rather a federation of kingdoms and principalities, so too, Wales was culturally diverse even within its own borders before incorporation into the United Kingdom. Nationalism arises as a response, not to internal beliefs, but against people identified as 'others'. In Nazi mythology, the German race was perceived as a pure-bred Aryan 'master race' and historians and archaeologists set out to prove that their race developed from the best of the classical world. So, too, within a nationalist framework, evidence is sought to support a point of view that legitimises this sense of self as different to others.

Colonialist

In the 1880s, Abbe Cauduban, a nineteenth-century archaeologist, spent five seasons excavating a cave in France searching for evidence of Old Stone Age habitation. Abbe found his evidence by digging carefully and methodically in the floor of the cave, all the time ignoring the paintings that covered the walls all around him. At that time, no one seriously believed that Stone Age man was capable of painting and so, to Abbe, the art could be safely ignored.

The colonialist framework emerged within the context of Victorian empire building. The take over of 'primitive' natives and the imposition of 'civilisation' was not only justified, it was a duty. Within this framework, aboriginal populations were viewed on a comparative continuum which judged them according to a model which assumed that human societies evolve through the same distinct periods of development. Even today, non-industrial peoples living a hunter/gatherer lifestyle are frequently referred to as having continued a 'stone-age' existence. Gamble (2004) offers the ruins of the great city of Zimbabwe as an example of colonialist ideas. African people, it was believed, were primitive and capable of only constructing mud huts. The existence of a sophisticated stone built city could mean only one thing – that European or Arab traders had reached the area long before the settlers arrived in what had become Rhodesia. The search was for evidence to prove who they were, where they had come from and when they had arrived. When Rhodesia gained independence the ruins became the symbol and the name of the new country, evidencing its pre-existing nationhood, and colonial ideas became nationalist ones.

Imperialist

There have been three great empires in the last century: Britain, the United States and the Soviet Union. Each has developed its own slant on the study of history and archaeology. Soviet studies tended to approach history from an economic viewpoint, which reflected Marxist principles, seeking evidence of inequalities and abuse of power by elites. The British adopted a more comparative stance in line with their colonialist ideology – comparing the achievements of various peoples over time. The Americans, meanwhile, led the way into what is now a generally accepted practice of scientific approach, but they, too, as an economic and cultural superforce, were able to dominate how history should be remembered – as Hollywood's somewhat relaxed approach to the depiction of history demonstrates.

These contexts and their significance for military history become apparent if we consider just one example. In January 1879, a well-armed British force was wiped out by a Zulu force at Isandhlwana (Saul 2004; Lock and Quantrill 2002). Failures on the part of (conveniently dead) quartermasters to dispense ammunition to the riflemen have been put forward as a significant factor in this shattering defeat for the British forces. It has been assumed that the Zulus, who, as native 'savages' were clearly unable to fight an organised battle, were able to overrun the camp by sheer force of numbers alone. Recent archaeological evidence has called this version into question and we need to ask whether, in fact, British failures led to their defeat or whether it might just be that they were outfought by a motivated, disciplined and well-led army. The implications for an ideology in which British might is used for the benefit of ignorant savages of a defeat by a native army fighting to protect their homes and families on behalf of a centralised system of power and control is immediately apparent.

PRIMARY SOURCES

By contrast, primary sources are more direct links to the events. They take the form of first-hand accounts, oral histories, reports and records unfiltered by any form of gatekeeping. Despite this, they too have their drawbacks.

The phrase 'I should know, I was there' is both an opportunity for the researcher to understand what it was like to participate in events and at the same time a warning to check what follows carefully. Anyone with military experience knows that the daily life of the ordinary man or woman in combat is one of confusion, rumour and counter-rumour mixed with terror, all taking place in a world that shrinks to the few hundred yards immediately around one's position. The soldier who, at the time of battle, is aware of the tactical and strategic situation and his part in it, is a rare soldier indeed. Hayward (2002) cites the example of Royal Air Force veterans of the Second World War who still talk of 'scarecrows'. These were said to be German flak shells designed to be fired at night, which mimicked the explosion of a fully laden bomber in order to demoralise the attacking aircrews. Hayward reports that no evidence of any such shell has been found and, in fact, what the crews really saw were exploding bombers. To force oneself to believe that such sights were fake is an obvious and understandable survival mechanism but one which, even if challenged years later, can be supported by the simple phrase, 'I should know, I was there'.

Nevertheless, these sources provide the researcher with a wealth of material from which to gather the basic details of times, dates, statistics and a myriad of facts alongside the personal and human experience of war. Professor Richard Holmes has argued that the 'historiography has long moved away from "scraps and chaps". Yet battles and the men who fought them are important; more so than we might wish to admit in an age when war's credibility as a means of pursuing political aims is increasingly questioned' (2003: 9). The continuing popularity of Professor Holmes' excellent accounts of the military shows that it is at this deeply personal level that war must be understood before we can really learn from it and, as he does, make real use of the words of the soldiers themselves as much as possible.

With these limitations in mind, we need to begin to explore what sources of information are available and how to use them effectively. Two main avenues need to be explored: the Internet and libraries/archives. For older readers, the Internet is a computerised system of retrieving information from a variety of sources whilst staying indoors and drinking tea. For younger readers, libraries and archives are older, dustier versions of the Internet in which you have to look things up in books yourself! You will need to use both at some stage.

GETTING STARTED

Sources can be as simple as watching a film or reading a novel about your chosen period. Often, this can have the added benefit of engaging other members of the family in your research and helping them to at least have some idea of why the empty field you've dragged them to is relevant. Unfortunately, the chances of finding what you need that easily are pretty slim.

Battlefield research is, in effect, detective work. You are trying to piece together an event long past using the evidence available to you. Some information is already known. Some is there, but hidden. Some will be lost forever. The key, then, is firstly to find out what you don't know. Chapter two discussed developing a research design to give structure to your work. Now, we need to look more closely at where information might be found.

Before setting out, you need to be organised. Make up two files – one for specific information directly relevant to what you want to do and one for other leads. This will mean that you will be able to keep focused and track your information. Develop a filing system within each file so that references can be easily found later. Remember that a seemingly irrelevant detail put to one side and lost will inevitably turn out to be the vital clue to the whole story.

FINDING SOURCES

There are literally thousands of collections of papers, photos and letters in homes and archives across the country and finding them all is an impossible task but finding enough need not be. The greatest problem is in identifying what sources are going to be needed to ensure that potentially expensive trips to records offices are kept to a minimum. It is also a matter of identifying what groups and individuals are already able to provide the information we need. Appendix C lists some of the resources and groups able to offer help and support to research projects, and the many genealogy guides available all offer advice on how to trace an individual.

Family archives

Many families have a shoebox filled with letters, medals and often photographs of members who have served in the forces. These can all be just as informative, often more so than official archives. They can be used to create the story of a real person through which to try to understand how they lived and died.

Medals

Whilst writing this section one of the authors had in front of him a First World War Victory Medal. Like most British campaign medals – those issued to all who took part in a particular theatre of operations – it is inscribed with the details of its recipient. In this case, '300100 Pte P Smith'. This is more than enough to begin to discover who he was and where he served.

Most soldiers who served with the British Army in the Great War qualified for campaign medals, normally the 1914 Star, 1914-15 Star, the British War Medal and the Victory Medal, commonly referred to as 'Pip, Squeak and Wilfred'. Those serving after 1915 would only be eligible for the British War Medal and Victory Medal, or 'Mutt and Jeff' as they came to be known. The Army Medals Office records soldiers' medal entitlement in lists known as 'Rolls'. These Rolls are linked to the Medal Card Index – the most complete existing list of British service personnel in the First World War. Although the medal cards themselves are now held by the Western Front Association, a long-term project has now completed the digitising of the Medal Index. You can now search free of charge online at the National Archives website (see addresses at the back of the book). The Index Card online provides the reference to where the soldier is listed on the Rolls.

The Medal Card will provide the soldier's name, rank and serial number, his regiment or corps, and occasionally, though not often, his unit. It may include his date of entry into a Theatre of War, especially in the early part of the war, the campaign medals he was awarded and the reference numbers that allow the soldier to be traced on the Medal Rolls.

The Medal Rolls themselves held at the National Archives (not yet available online) can give further information about a soldier, such as the battalion in which he served, that will allow further research to be undertaken. This is helpful for regiments of the infantry and cavalry, but less so for the larger corps such as the Royal Artillery, Royal Engineers and Army Service Corps where soldiers might have moved between units as the need arose.

Other, more recent, records are harder to trace, as they remain with the Ministry of Defence. However, with a good reference guide, you should be able to identify medals quite easily and, if they are inscribed, you will be able to use this information to narrow your search considerably. Even if you do not have the medal itself, but only the ribbon usually worn in its place, this will at least allow you to identify the award.

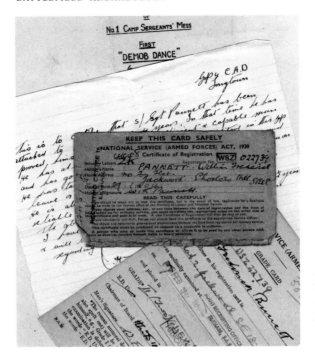

Left and below: 29 and *30* The type of material commonly found in a family archive. Evidence such as ration cards, pay books, discharge papers or medals can all provide clues to the story. *Tim Lynch collection*

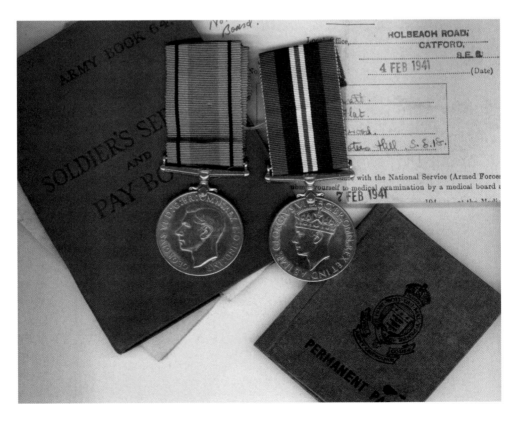

Photographs

Often the most poignant of artefacts, photos remind us of the serviceman as a person. Many had portraits taken after joining the forces and some took cameras with them on active service. With practice, the clues these contain will become obvious and allow you to identify roughly the stage of a persons' career and something about where they were taken.

An excellent guide to interpreting First World War period photos is Ian Swinnerton's *Identifying Your WW1 Soldier from Badges and Photographs* (available via the Western Front Association and specialist booksellers). In it, he describes what to look for and how to use the information. Although it focuses on 1914-18, the guide holds true for other periods too.

Letters

Letters are a vital link for anyone on active service with 'normality' back home. The arrival of the mail is the most eagerly anticipated event of the day. During the Falklands War, RAF Hercules transport aircraft dropped mail canisters into the sea by parachute for collection by naval ships. When the RAF crews heard criticism from their naval colleagues that their role was unimportant, they arranged for a drop to go wrong. A canister containing scrap paper was allowed to fall open as it left the aircraft, scattering

31 All soldiers like souvenirs of their travels, even under the wrong circumstances. Here a group of German soldiers relax somewhere in France. Photos like these often turn up at militaria fairs or through specialist dealers. *Tim Lynch collection*

hundreds of pieces of paper into the sea near a waiting ship. The ship's crew watched their only link with home apparently disappear beneath the waves before the Hercules made a second pass and made the real drop. There were no more complaints.

For the families back home, letters were proof that a loved one was alive but families were painfully aware that each letter might be the last. As a result many were kept – each one added to a growing pile providing a lasting journal of the war as seen by one man. It is these sources that provide some of the most telling details of the best military histories.

THE INTERNET

Chapter two looked at research design and the need to clarify what the project was intended to achieve. Now we need to consider what information is needed to make a start.

Imagine that you want to trace a history of your great uncle's service. You know he was in the Grenadier Guards and later served with the King's Own Yorkshire Light Infantry (KOYLI) in the 9th Battalion. You may decide to search the Internet using keywords like 'guards'. Google, one of the largest search engines, will offer you a choice of 37,800,000 pages containing the word 'guards'. You may decide to use 'grenadier' instead and will only get 2,300,000 pages to choose from. Combining the two choices, narrows your results down to just 463,000 pages. You decide to check out the other connection. King's Own Yorkshire Light Infantry is available on 91,600 pages (more if the search engine picks out individual words). You decide to try adding '9' to the mix in order to find the 9th Battalion. This returns 66,900 pages. And, '9th', plus 'King's Own Yorkshire Light Infantry', brings 50,000 pages. The '9th battalion' added to 'King's Own Yorkshire Light Infantry' finds 26,900 matches. Rewriting it as '9th King's Own Yorkshire Light Infantry' brings just two matches – neither of which are what you need.

By spending a few minutes clarifying your search, you can increase your chances of finding what you need, fast and effectively. Before you start, consider what you want from your search:

1 Do you want a specific hard-to-find document on a specialised subject or general information on a broader topic? Do you need to search the entire Web? Is what you are seeking likely to be found on a number of sites or only the most popular sites?
2 If you are looking for general information, do you need to look for a directory rather than a website? (A directory will list sites and forums according to specific interests). A directory like *Yahoo!*, for example, may help you to access a group offering information on your chosen field.
3 Are you looking for information that might be contained within another database? The 1901 Census is available free online and contains details of everyone in the country at that time, but you will only access the information through its own searchable database. The Commonwealth War Graves Commission's site includes

32 German trench in use, 1916

huge amounts of information, but you can only access it through their designated search.

4 Is the information you are looking for likely to be in a page's title or first paragraph, or buried deeper within the document or site? Is the information going to be part of the title (as in 'A history of the Bloggs family 1300-1900') or is it going to be tucked away within a wider history ('A history of Bloggshire families')?

5 Choose your search method with these factors in mind. Often working from the broadest information base and focusing in is the easiest and most effective method.

Using a sheet of paper, begin to draw up the following:

Step 1: State what you want to find

First, in one or two sentences, state what you want to find on the Internet. For example:

> I want to find information on my local regiment's part in the Napoleonic wars.
> What would my great uncle have done during his military service?
> Local tradition says a battle took place near here. Where did it happen?

Step 2: Identify keywords

Next, underline the main concepts in the statement.

> I want to find information on my <u>local regiment</u> in the <u>Napoleonic</u> wars.

What would my <u>great uncle</u> have done during his <u>military service</u>?

Local tradition says <u>a battle took place near here.</u> Where did it happen?

This allows you to focus in on the relevant keywords that will narrow down the parameters of your search.

Step 3: Look for variations on your keywords and other forms of wording

Consider other ways of phrasing the questions. For example, in the British Army a soldier may hold the rank of Private and be known as Private Smith. Being the wonderfully weird organisation that it is, he could, depending on what unit he serves with, equally be known as Guardsman, Rifleman, Fusilier, Kingsman, Marine, Trooper, Driver, Gunner, Signaller, Craftsman or Bandsman Smith. Consider these variations along with how this might be written down. British soldiers may be abbreviated as 'Pte', Americans as 'Pvt'.

In 1914, a 'Pals' Battalion was formed in a few hours at a recruiting office set up in the Glasgow Tramsheds. The battalion rejoiced in the title of the 15th (Service) Battalion Highland Light Infantry (City Of Glasgow Corporation Tramways). In East Yorkshire, the city of Hull produced four battalions, including the 10th Battalion, East Yorkshire Regiment, made up of men from shops and known as the Hull Commercials; the 11th Battalion from businesses and known as the Hull Tradesmen; the 12th, comprising men from football and rugby teams, sports clubs and local gyms, who became the Hull Sportsmen; and the 13th, known simply as Hull t'others. All these units were known by their official title, nicknames, battalion numbers or any combination of these. Consider searching each name, either separately or as a search string (see below).

What local tradition describes as a 'battle' may also be described as a 'skirmish', 'fight', 'siege', an 'assault', 'attack', 'ambush' or a 'retreat'. Consider alternative descriptions of the event.

Even in a fairly specific search, you need to leave room for information that almost, but not quite, matches the criteria you put into the computer.

Step 4: Combine the variations, synonyms, keywords and variant word forms

By using what are known as Boolean Operatives, you can combine combinations of words into what are known as search strings to help eliminate irrelevant pages. Not all search engines accept the following but most will either use these or offer an 'Advanced Search' option which will perform much the same function.

The most common Boolean Operation is to enclose the phrase you are looking for in double quotation marks (such as "Grenadier Guards"). This will search for that exact phrase. Unfortunately, if the webpage has a variation on that or a spelling mistake, it will not be picked up and you may miss useful information.

Using the + symbol or AND/OR (always in capitals and leaving a space between words – such as 'Grenadier Guards' AND Germany). The AND operator instructs the search engine to search for all documents containing both the exact phrase and any key words you specify. The OR operator instructs the search engine to search for documents containing either key word you specify.

In the same way, using NOT allows you to narrow a search by specifying what you are NOT looking for. The NOT operator excludes documents containing a key word you specify. Some search engines use the '−' symbol as the operator, which works the same way as in 'Grenadier Guards'+ Germany NOT Austria.

Having specified that you are looking for pages containing information on the 'Grenadier Guards' and their service in Germany, you may find that a page is displayed in which a passing mention of the Grenadier Guards is linked with a totally unconnected reference to Germany in a completely separate part of a website. This can often happen but the use of the 'Advanced Search' option may allow the use of other tools to narrow the search further.

NEAR/ADJ operators are used by more advanced search engines to look for key words in a certain proximity to another key word. For example, the NEAR operator would look for 'Grenadier Guards' NEAR Germany and usually defaults to within twenty-five words. You can change the proximity to within 5 words by using NEAR/5, or any other number of words you choose. Most search engines do not check for word order, so 'Grenadier Guards' could be within five words before or after Germany. The ADJ operator stands for 'adjacent'. This operator will return only documents in which, say, George is adjacent to Washington. ADJ is more strict than NEAR and will return fewer hits.

Another method of specifying particular searches is to use parenthesis. This is especially useful where there may be variations on a keyword. For example, the King's Own Yorkshire Light Infantry are often referred to simply as KOYLI. By using parentheses and the OR operative, you can instruct the computer to search for both. Parentheses work in a similar fashion to the way they are used in mathematics, by setting up groups of operations that must be performed before other parts of the whole can be completed. Parentheses can be used to filter all sorts of lists and can be combined with most search operators. So you could use '(King's Own Yorkshire Light Infantry OR KOYLI) AND 1945 NEAR/5 Rhine'. This will search for both types of reference to the regiment and then search for the date within five words of the word 'Rhine' and should produce reasonably useful results.

Step 5: Check your spelling

Search engines return websites with words that match your keywords. If you misspell a keyword, your results will only contain websites where that word is also misspelled.

Because the search engine will be specific, you also need to allow for variations in a spelling. 'Wildcards' using the ★ symbol allow this. A search for 'General Patton's command centre' will return British based sites. It will not pick up American sites in which 'centre' is written as 'center'. To get around this problem, enter 'General Patton's command cent★★' and both forms will be displayed. In summary:

1 Enter synonyms, alternate spellings and alternate forms (such as fight, fighting, fought) for your search terms.
2 Enter all the singular or unique terms which are likely to be included in the document or site you are seeking.

3 Avoid using very common terms (such as battle, soldiers) which may lead to potentially millions of irrelevant search results.

4 Use the 'help' feature to determine how your search engine uses capitals and plurals, and enter capitalized or plural forms of your search words if appropriate.

5 Use a phrase or proper name if possible to narrow your search and therefore retrieve more relevant results (unless you want a large number of results).

6 Pay attention to proper spacing and punctuation in your search syntax (i.e. no space when using + means +battle not + battle).

Remember that the Internet is an international tool. It is always worth searching in other languages, especially on French sites if you want information on the World Wars. Many provide an automatic translation but even where this is not available, some search engines such as *AltaVista* provide a translation feature. With this service French, German, Italian, Spanish and Portuguese websites are translated to English and vice-versa.

To use this capability, enter your keywords and click the Search button at either the Simple or Advanced Search page. When the search results appear, click the Translate link at the bottom of the result of interest.

Favourites

Whenever you find a site that appears useful you have two options. You can save the site to your computer by clicking on 'File' on the toolbar, then 'Save' in the dropdown box that will appear. This will then save the page to a folder you choose. It is a good idea to have one for each topic you are researching and to keep a note of where the webpage can be found, either by recording what search you used to find it or by noting the web address displayed at the top of the page. Alternatively, by using the 'Favorite Places' tool on the top of the screen, you can 'bookmark' the webpage and return to it quickly. This feature is especially useful for Forum sites where the content may change or you may need to visit regularly to check for updates.

ARCHIVES AND LIBRARIES

Although potentially costly to use in terms of travel and time, archives and libraries are a vital part of the process. The Internet is a wonderful tool but there is an enormous amount of information out there that has never been catalogued properly, let alone digitised. A few years ago, a researcher uncovered a previously unknown Shakespeare sonnet in a library collection simply by looking up 'Shakespeare' on an old card index and following the reference to a dusty old box containing original manuscripts. For anyone interested in military history, a trip to a regimental archive can be akin to being a child let loose in a toy shop.

It can also be an incredibly frustrating experience. Handwritten accounts of battles stop abruptly where the second page has been lost, the date that you need will inevitably be missing from the war diary and the document you think will answer all your questions, having driven 100 miles to see, will contain nothing you don't already know. That is why using the Internet can be effective as the first step in the process. It will allow you to identify possible sources of information and either have copies made and sent to you or at least be able to get a better idea of what is available.

The process for using a library or archive is very similar to what we have already done. Start by identifying what it is you need from the trip and what keywords you need to check. Using card indexes is similar to using keyword searches on the Internet, you need to consider alternatives. A search for a battalion by number may not be successful, a search for 'Bloggshire Pals' may produce vast amounts.

Most archives require that researchers use only pencils when working to prevent damage to the documents and it is worth making sure you have spares. Many also allow the use of digital cameras. This is an excellent way of keeping costs down, by photographing lengthy documents for examination later. Always include a shot of your notebook with the document reference so you can find it again later if necessary.

Reading and interpreting documents

There will inevitably come a time when the neatly-typed source material runs out and you will need to have at least a basic understanding of the arcane art of reading old handwriting. Paleography is the art of interpreting handwritten documents and it is a skill that needs practice. Until the invention of the typewriter, all documents were completed by hand prior to being set in print and many official records remain handwritten. Understanding the different styles is vital to understanding the material. Three main styles are common:

Secretary hand

From the fifteenth century, secretary hand was used for legal documents and remained in use for over 300 years. It can be confusing. Capital letters, for example, are produced with decorative flourishes that can make reading names difficult. In particular, the capital F is often represented as 'ff' – hence some families may claim to be called 'ffolke' or 'ffiennes' because this is how it appears to be written. Most lower case letters are recognisable but may have some variations such as:

- 'c' can look like the modern 'r'.
- 'e' in the middle of a word may look like 'c' but at the end of the word may look like a modern 'e' reversed.
- 's' at the end of a word may be represented as a circle with an upward stroke.
- 'th' may be written as 'y' (as in 'ye olde') but not in the middle of a word.
- 'w' may be written as 'iv'.

Dates often appear in their Latin versions and may be confusing. The current tax year works from April because, until the seventeenth century, this was regarded as the New Year. Hence, a document dated 'Martii 1639' will probably mean March 1640 ('probably' because the modern dating system was phased in over several decades and sometimes

33 A message home from the front lines. *Tim Lynch collection*

documents may appear to be a year apart but are actually contemporary). You need to consider how this may affect your understanding of the timeline for events.

Italic

Italic handwriting was introduced in the sixteenth century and, being easier than secretary hand, was considered suitable for use by women. Elizabeth I was taught Italic as a child, and the system gained popularity among the upper classes before gradually becoming more widely used. It is relatively easy to read and found in private papers and later in parish records.

Copperplate

Copperplate came into use around 1700 and was named after the writing used in book illustrations, produced by engravers on copper plates for printing. It is easy to read and should not present too many problems for the researcher.

In each case, there are sometimes wide variations in how a word is spelled – often with two or more versions of a name within the same document. Prior to the nineteenth century, spelling was a matter of personal choice and so it is often a good idea to photocopy the document for translation at home. Where a word appears difficult to read, try breaking it down into its individual letters, then read them aloud. Bear in mind the local accent and how this might affect the way the word was used and thus written. When translating a document, number each line on the copy and on your translation so that you can refer more easily to particular words if necessary.

Courses may be available locally through history departments or family history groups to guide you through the basics of palaeography and genealogy resource centres can provide guides to handwriting, words and terms likely to be found. In more recent documents, the writing may be clear but jargon and abbreviations make it difficult to interpret. In that case, do not be afraid to make use of Internet forums where members often take great pleasure in leading novices through the sometimes frustrating process of translating military records into plain English.

The use of two case studies will demonstrate how these different sources can be used to support each other and to add pieces to the puzzle. Both are based on work in the same geographical area but cover two very different periods. They are based on research using a local library – in this case the public library of Barnsley, South Yorkshire – to show that it is not necessary to have access to the major archives to find what you are looking for. The library at Barnsley is typical of hundreds of similar establishments and contains the same types of material available throughout the country. The following studies were both completed using the most basic resources available locally.

Looking for a fight? Finding a forgotten battlefield

Earlier, we looked at how unreliable sources can be in respect of lesser-known battlefields. This example follows the process of identifying one of the many 'lost' battlefields of the English Civil Wars.

The battle of Tankersley Moor is just one of the hundreds of barely remembered fights across the country in the sporadic, but often violent, conflicts that erupted throughout the nation during the decade of upheaval variously known as the English Civil War, the Great Rebellion or the Wars of the Three Kingdoms. Between 1642 and 1652 thousands of homes were destroyed and many thousands of people died as fighting came to towns and villages across the British Isles, with an estimated 50,000 Royalist and 34,000 Parliamentarian soldiers killed in more than 500 known engagements, mostly in the years before 1649. Perhaps another 100,000 died of disease in the same period. With a few highly publicised exceptions, the actions that caused these deaths are anonymous episodes, remembered, if at all, only as local traditions.

Lying just south of Barnsley on the M1 motorway, Tankersley today is a barely noticeable suburb, most of whose residents are unaware that they live on the scene of a battle during the English Civil Wars. Local tradition of the Tankersley area, gleaned from a variety of sources, tells us that Sir Francis Wortley of nearby Wortley Hall was an ardent Royalist who raised a force of 900 men from his estate to fight the Parliamentary Army on the moor in 1647. During the battle, Tankersley Hall was destroyed and Sir Francis taken prisoner. He died in the Tower of London some years later. A cart at Wortley Forge Industrial Museum is said to have been used by his forces at Tankersley and at Marston Moor. Unfortunately, as so often with local tradition, there are a few errors – 'he didn't, it wasn't, he wasn't and the date is wrong'. The cart, fully original except for the replaced wheels and extensive refurbishment of the body, is first recorded to have been used in 1647, four years after Tankersley and three years after Marston Moor. One source, having stated (correctly) that Wortley was captured at the siege of Walton House, then immediately claims that the boots he wore at the battle of Marston Moor were on display at Wortley Hall, ignoring that fact that it had already said that he was a prisoner at the Tower of London at the time of that battle. Stories like this are to be found all around the country – a mixture of half-remembered fact, legend and supposition. In many ways it is understandable that, in an age when literacy levels were low, accurate recording of events was unlikely, but the same problems persist even now.

The local evidence

The traditional account is obviously unreliable as it is presented, but there is at least something behind it since there is some hard evidence to be found. More detailed local histories are equally frustrating. Writing a history of nearby Worsbrough in 1872, Joseph Wilkinson referred to a local man, Mr Bashforth, who 'could relate no small amount of traditionary lore touching the exploits of Cromwell and his Army at Houndhill, Stainborough, Tankersley, and the surrounding villages'. Unfortunately, he does not appear to have considered any of this lore worth recording. A few years later, the first recorded physical evidence surfaced in 1876, when an Ash tree near the church was cut down and a 'musket ball' found. (The description given is of a bullet, 1½in long, hollow for half its length, which suggests that it may, in fact, be the cap of a powder flask. Unfortunately, the item has disappeared again). Then, in 1917, canonballs were apparently discovered along Tankersley Lane. Clearly then a fight of some sort had taken place here.

Although the story is known locally, no serious research into the battle appears to have been undertaken. An Internet search revealed just two accounts of the battle, one by Simon Wright, who portrays one of Newcastle's Whitecoats as a member of the Sealed Knot re-enactment society and the other, heavily based on Mr Wright's account, by wargamer Noel Williams. Neither make any claim to be historians and so the material is not intended as anything other than an attempt to open discussion about the battle, but Mr Wright does at least point the way. The first step, then, is to establish which, if any, of the known details are reliable.

Sir Francis Wortley

An Internet search for Sir Francis, and variations on his name, produced a mixed bag of information. At least three different men were identified over three generations and so biographical information was found for each to determine which was the most likely candidate. The Sir Francis usually discussed in relation to the Civil Wars is the man most often remembered as a poet and writer. He was created a baronet in 1611, sat as MP for Retford in the 1620s and was a close friend of the Earl of Strafford. A portrait of him was found through a website selling old prints and a rough life history could be sketched out. He was a noted Royalist and, if a battle did take place, he would have had a leading role.

Tankersley

The local church has a small collection of cannonballs found nearby and there is one brief mention of a battle by the Marquis of Newcastle's wife in her biography of him.

Above: 34 Tankersley church. The building was in existence at the time of the battle and so we can orientate around it to identify where forces may have been

Right: 35 Sir Francis Wortley. *Tim Lynch collection*

Using these facts as a starting point, searches were carried out on the Internet and in the local history archives of Barnsley library. Secondary sources were used to establish the context of the battle, the training, logistics and deployment of troops and the background information against which it was possible to draw conclusions from the primary sources available.

Using sources available in the public lending library and by one trip to nearby Bradford to consult their copy of Peter Newman's 'Royalist Army in the North' (York PhD Thesis 1978), it was possible to piece together a fairly detailed history. All the following information is taken either from secondary sources about the civil wars in general or from copies of local archive material transcribed by amateur historians and placed in the library's collections. Geographical details are taken from copies of original maps and using the techniques described in chapter four.

In January 1642, after years of increasing bitterness between the King and Parliament, Charles I headed north to York to set up a military base independent of Parliamentary restraint. It was the culmination of a decade in which Charles had refused to allow Parliament to encroach on what he saw as his divine right to rule absolutely. In 1639, he brought the country to the brink of war with Scotland and only last minute negotiations prevented any real fighting. Another brief war the following year saw Charles lead his English Army to defeat at Newburn but he broke the royal finances in doing so. When, shortly after the English Army had been demobilised from this second war, rebellion broke out in Ireland, Charles reluctantly turned to Parliamentary revenue to fund a new military expedition. Parliament was concerned that a well-equipped Army under the command of the king could be used against them if he were truly determined to exercise absolutionist power. Rebellion against the King at this time was unthinkable, but Parliamentary members determined to restrain the King by removing the support of his 'evil counsellors'. Chief among these dangerous men was Thomas Wentworth, the Earl of Strafford, a Yorkshireman from Wentworth Woodhouse in South Yorkshire who enjoyed popular support among the local gentry. His impeachment and trial for treason, orchestrated by enemies within Parliament, culminated in his execution in 1641 and drove the wedge between the King and Parliament that would lead to war.

As he moved north, the King and Parliament were locked in a struggle for control of the local militia. Parliament had used the Militia Ordnance to confuse the issue so instead, at his northern stronghold in York, Charles reintroduced the medieval Commission of Array. First introduced in 1327 and last used in 1557, the commission was intended to counter foreign invasion and gave the commissioners empowered by the King the authority to call up all able-bodied men for military service. Those unfit to serve were required to contribute to the upkeep of the army through taxation. The noted historian Peter Newman said:

> The first specifically military development in the north, predating the commission of May
> 11th, seems to have come from a local justice of the peace, Sir Francis Wortley. According
> to a report, he unambiguously drew his sword on May 3rd and publicly declared for the
> king, and by the 12th was recruiting 200 gentlemen to form a Royal Lifeguard of Horse.

36 Cannonballs, Tankersley church

A Trainband infantry regiment was also brought in as a Lifeguard, that of Sir Robert Strickland.

Wortley, a close friend and near neighbour of Thomas Wentworth is, as we have already established, central to the story that follows.

In February 1642, Charles' catholic wife, Henrietta Maria, had been sent to Holland to procure weapons and military experts. To facilitate her return, Charles intended to seize the arsenal at Hull and to use the port as his supply base. His failure to secure Hull after several attempts meant that instead he was forced to turn to the ports further up the north-east coast and called upon William Cavendish, the Earl of Newcastle, to secure these for him. Initially, Newcastle's role was simply to provide a safe landing place for Henrietta Maria and the supplies she would bring but by July 1642, Charles had conferred on him the generalship of all Royalist forces north of the Trent and gave him wide powers to raise troops, grant commissions and even knighthoods. After securing agreements about the funding of his force, Newcastle crossed into Yorkshire to secure the county for the king.

There followed a campaign that saw Newcastle's forces push back the Parliamentary forces under the command of Ferdinando and Thomas Fairfax into pockets of fierce resistance among what would become the mill towns of West Yorkshire but throughout, Newcastle's priority remained that of ensuring the safe passage of the Queen and her supplies to the King's army at Oxford. Newcastle has been criticised for his failure to follow through his early successes, but the safe arrival of Henrietta Maria at York in March 1643 diverted his attention away from securing the defeat of the Fairfaxes and towards the defence of York in order to prepare the way south. The first convoy of 1500 men and weapons left the city in April 1643. The chain of events that led to Tankersley Moor had been set in motion.

Writing about this period, Hilaire Belloc commented:

> … the numbers engaged upon either side of the struggle were usually small. Skirmishes outside country houses are dignified by the name of sieges; a mêlée of a few horse is often called a battle, while the lack of plan and purpose in much of the fighting makes the general observer underrate, if anything, the position of this English episode in the general military history of the seventeenth century.

Before embarking on a search for the battle of Tankersley Moor, or indeed any battle of this period, we need, considering Belloc's comments, firstly to establish whether there actually is a battle to seek. If, as he suggests, 'actions' of this period may be no more than one group of youths with bad hairstyles indulging in a slinging match with their floppy-hatted neighbours, what evidence do we have that a significant fight took place?

The only direct contemporary source we have for the battle comes from the Duchess of Newcastle's memoirs of her husband. At the end of March 1643, the Royalists had routed the enemy at Seacroft Moor near Leeds and had taken about 800 prisoners.

> Immediately after, in pursuit of that victory, my lord sent a considerable party into the West of Yorkshire, where they met with about 2,000 of the enemy's forces, taken out of their several garrisons in those parts to execute some design upon a moor called Tankersley Moor, and there fought them, and routed them; many were slain, and some taken prisoners.

This would appear to place the battle in early April. However, the Duchess would seem to have made a slight error in her chronology. In the immediate aftermath of Seacroft Moor, Newcastle advanced against Leeds with the intention of taking the town but, after a short bombardment, deferred to his deputy, James King, and instead shifted his attention to the capture and consolidation of nearby Wakefield.

Once the garrison was established, the Duchess reports:

> … receiving intelligence that in two market towns southwest from Wakefield viz Rotherham and Sheffield, the enemie was very busie to raise forces against his majesty and had fortified them both about four miles distant from each other hoping thereby to give protection and encouragement to all those parts of the country which were populous rich and rebellious, he thought it necessary to use his best endeavours in April 1643 to march with part of his Army from Wakefield into the mentioned parts, attended with a train of artillery and ammunition, leaving the greatest part of it in Wakefield.

Newcastle's men began to advance south toward their targets and Royalist forces took control of Barnsley, roughly halfway between Wakefield and Rotherham. On 20 April, Sir Thomas Fairfax reported to his father:

… some of the Penistone men came also to demand aid, there being seventeen colours in Barnsley, five miles of them. I advised them to seek help from Rotherham and Sheffield, and whilst they stood upon their guards to get their goods to places of most safeguard, for it will be impossible without more horse to defend the county from spoil.

Waiting for Newcastle's men at Barnsley were infantry, dragoons and horse raised by Wortley and other local gentry and currently garrisoned at his own house and nearby Tankersley Hall.

Fairfax's advice to the Parliamentary garrison at Penistone seems to have been heeded and the Royalist newssheet *Mercurius Aulicus*, in a report dated 6 May 1643, describes:

… the Earle of Newcastles forces in the North encountered … with a body of the Rebels, consisting of 3000 men (which were going, as it is conceived, to the relief of Leeds) & had so fortunate successe therein, that they totally routed the whole body of them, 150 of them being killed in the place, 240 prisoners taken.

From this, we can tentatively date the battle in the last week or so of April, with corroborating evidence for the date coming from an entry in the Barnsley Parish Registers dated 1 May 1643, which records the burial of 'Luke Carleil, Willm Dobson, Luke Garfield soldiers', several days before the next known action in the area, the attack on Rotherham on 4 May. In nearby Sheffield, the burials of three men, one identified only as 'a soulgier', are recorded as having taken place on 6 May, a date two days before the attack on Sheffield began . It is possible that these men, too, were casualties of the battle.

By late April, the Royalist Army in the north had forced a wedge across Yorkshire, from the north-east to the south-west of the county. York, Pontefract, Wakefield and Doncaster were all in Newcastle's hands. In Hull, Sir John Hotham was seriously reconsidering his decision to hold the port for Parliament. In the West Riding mill towns of Leeds, Bradford, Halifax and Huddersfield, the Fairfaxes were besieged and rapidly running out of resources to reinforce outlying districts, such as the garrison of Penistone at the southern extremity of this enclave. To the south, Rotherham and Sheffield Castle were both held by Parliament and threatened the safety of any convoy traveling beyond the county. These latter garrisons could be reinforced from Nottinghamshire and Derbyshire respectively and, as Newcastle's men advanced on Rotherham, the Parliamentary commander in Derbyshire, Sir John Gell, was assembling a force equipped with cannon to do just that. Further afield, Cromwell was drawing up plans for a relief column to be sent to support the Fairfaxes. The plan was abandoned after Hotham's son, now committed to changing sides, wrote to assure Cromwell that the force was no longer needed.

Across the Pennines in Lancashire, the hundreds of Blackburn and Salford had declared for Parliament from the outset. These towns bordered on the Parliamentary enclaves in Yorkshire and the old Roman roads that led across the moors to Bradford, Penistone and Sheffield made them an obvious choice to supply reinforcements. Fairfax had expected the arrival of troops from Lancashire by 20 April and by the time of the

Adwalton Moor battle, 1600 troops had joined him from across the border. In south-west Yorkshire, the only thing standing between the southern forces and the West Riding towns was the garrison established by Sir Francis Wortley at Tankersley and in his own home, Wortley Hall. Against this background, the order from Fairfax to the Penistone garrison and the report in *Mercurius Aulicus* both support the theory that a force, probably from Rotherham, was advancing to break through to Penistone in order to link up the two armies.

In addition to the linking of the forces, such an attack could have another important aim. Tankersley sits atop a seam of ironstone and since the thirteenth century it had been mined to feed the local iron industry. The Wortley family's fortunes were closely tied to ironworking, owning as they did forges in the Wharncliffe valley, at Wortley itself and as far north as Halifax. Within a few miles of Tankersley, major forges were in operation at Kimberworth, Wadsley and Wortley Top and all are known to have been involved in weapons manufacture during this period. Capturing or destroying these could seriously impede the ammunition-starved Royalist army's advance or at least hamper the expected siege of Sheffield Castle.

Finally, the destruction of the Wortley garrison and the family's business interests would have been of great personal satisfaction to Sir John Gell, who had secured Sheffield Castle in October 1642 and who commanded forces in neighbouring Derbyshire. Gell had clashed with Sir Francis Wortley's troopers several times during their incursions into his territory throughout that autumn.

Although military service abroad was widespread among the gentry, where combat experience in the wars then engulfing Europe was considered in much the same way as 'the Great Tour' was to be viewed in later generations, in Britain itself over a century of peace had weakened the military. In theory, under the principle of *posse comitatus*, every able-bodied man between the ages of 16 and 60 was eligible for call-up by the county sheriff if invasion threatened. This was essentially a local defence force, poorly (if at all) trained and armed, and which proved difficult to persuade to fight outside local boundaries.

Alongside these, 'trained bands' were created to form what historian John Barratt calls 'a socially and politically reliable force in case of rebellion'. Such recruits were to be 'men sufficient, of able and active bodies; none of the meaner sort or servants; but only such as be of the Gentrie, Free-holders, and good Farmers, or their sonnes, that are likely to be resident'. These local trained bands were to become the backbone of the armies in the early stages of the war. At Barnsley, a muster roll of 1587 shows that Sir Francis Wortley's father commanded the band there. Among those listed is one John Jenkyngson, and the signing of Francis Wortley's orders by one Anthony Jenkinson is probably not pure coincidence – these forces tended toward developing a strong local, almost family character.

Relations between the trained bands and the population were sometimes strained. In the summer of 1641, at Stainborough near Barnsley, a trooper, Francis White, was killed in an altercation with locals. His killer, a man named Benton, was committed to York. We don't know his ultimate fate but we do know he was still being held in 1643.

37 Fast, mobile and tough, dragoons like Wortley's acted as a kind of Special Forces unit

These, then, were the forces upon which the newly appointed commanders could draw. Often, the commissions granted by either side were overly optimistic in their expectations of the willingness of local able-bodied men to give up their farms and businesses for an unspecified length of time. Wortley was to find to his embarrassment later that year when the local population failed to provide even half of the 500 men he was tasked to form into an infantry regiment.

Turning now to the more specific opposing armies, we do not know the exact size or composition of the force that left Wakefield, but the Fairfax letter states 'seventeen colours' in Barnsley by late April. If these were infantry, it would indicate a force of 1500 and perhaps as high as 2000 men. Even if these were smaller units of Horse, it would still represent a sizable force, growing as local garrisons and trained bands appear to have linked up with the force.

At the core, though, two regiments seem to be prime candidates for forming the convoy. Sir William Savile of Thornhill, near Wakefield, had had close ties with the Earl of Strafford and now had established a regiment from his estates across the region. Savile, later appointed Governor of Sheffield Castle, was of a family who had historic links with the Tankersley area and would therefore be a logical choice of commander. His uncle, Sir John Savile, of Lupset near Wakefield, was a strong supporter of Parliament and had already made an enemy of Francis Wortley when the two men had fought a duel in 1626. Peter Newman's analysis of the Northern Army places Colonel George Wentworth's Regiment of Foot in Wakefield and this could also make them a sensible choice. Wentworth, a kinsman of Thomas Wentworth, was from the Woolley area, approximately a third of the distance between the garrison at Wakefield and Tankersley, and so would know the area and people well.

Newman cites a muster roll found in the Wentworth family archives which describes seventy-one men in three 'rankes'. This, he argues, would normally be suggestive of a cavalry unit and asks whether the roll may relate to either Savile's regiment or a pre-war trained band muster. The presence of John Oxley, Thomas English, Nicholas Burkley and Henry Carrington in the list of the 'third ranke' is noted in a 1907 history of Barnsley, supporting the view that these men were prominent local citizens of the Militia. In any case, if these men were in Yorkshire, their local knowledge and connections would make them the obvious choice to lead the attack.

Of the troops and commanders available to Newcastle, only Sir Francis Wortley and his dragoons are known with any certainty to have been part of the force. Wortley, as we have seen, was the first to raise forces for the king when he established a unit of 200 Horse to act as the King's Lifeguard. This force went with the Royalist Army and seems to have made something of a nuisance of itself, earning a special mention in Hotham's report to Parliament. From here, it may be that Wortley took part in the Edgehill campaign. Certainly we can place his force in Warwickshire in October 1642 and in November of that year, Wortley was implicated in complaints of plunder from Shropshire, Staffordshire, Cheshire and Derbyshire.

Returning home, he fortified his own Wortley Hall and the nearby Tankersley Hall. A warrant dated late in 1642 tells us:

> Whereas, on the establishment of the garrison commanded by Sir Francis Wortley, knight and baronet, at Tankersley or thereabouts, agreed upon the two and twentieth day of July last past, and subscribed by his Excellencie the Earl of Newcastle, the several parishes enumerated are appointed to pay to the said Sir Francis Wortley, for the mainteynance of his said garrison (which is to consist of one hundred and fiftie dragoons besides officers) the sum of eighty-five pounds fifteen shillings five pence farthinge by the weeke.

At first inspection, Sir Francis, like many of his contemporaries, appears to have been remarkably long lived and robust, until closer examination of the family tree reveals that care needs to be taken when examining records based solely on the name of the individual. The Francis Wortley who attended Mary Queen of Scots during her long imprisonment at Sheffield is not the same one as the man who drew his sword at York or who bequeathed his estate to his illegitimate daughter in 1668. In fact, Sir Francis was the grandson of Francis Wortley and was created baronet in 1611, at the age of 19. His son, also named Sir Francis, is described by Martyn Bennett as having been a cavalry commander under Henry Hastings. So we can begin to make some separation between the 50-year-old local commander and his 22-year-old cavalry officer son. From the sources available, it would seem to have been the elder man who fought at Tankersley Moor.

Having established garrisons at Tankersley and Wortley, Sir Francis enthusiastically set about raising taxes and assessments against the local population, ranging so far afield that he drew complaints from the commander of the Royalist garrison at Pontefract Castle. The Puritan diarist Oliver Heywood writes of Wortley having 'roved up and down the country robbing and taxing many honest people'. Spencer writes of him as 'the most troublesome in the district for besides being a thorn in the flesh of the local Parliamentary forces, he levied lays and assessments on both friend and foe alike'. In fact, it appears that tax collecting was more a hobby than a military necessity for Wortley – the legend of *The Dragon of Wantley* is, in fact, based on a satirical account of his dispute with tenants over church taxes.

Somewhat confusingly, Wortley appears in the lists of Royalist officers as having commanded Horse, dragoon and Foot units. We have seen that he raised a unit of Horse at the outbreak of war and garrisoned his local commands with dragoons. His attempts to raise infantry, as we will see, were somewhat less successful. Nevertheless Wortley appears to have been almost a stereotypically dashing, enthusiastic and committed cavalier commander in this crucial stage of the war.

If we know little about the Royalist force, we know even less about the Parliamentary troops facing them. In October 1642, Sir John Gell had taken Sheffield Castle for Parliament and set John Bright to work recruiting for the garrison. Things do not appear to have gone well and by September 1642, a report talks of Gell being 'importuned to help there at Sheaffield to suppress a muteny there' (although another source shifts this to a place called Wheatfield). We do know, however, that Sheffield was later surrendered without resistance, thus calling into question the ability of the garrison to send out an aggressive force.

Rotherham, by contrast, appears to have taken its support of Parliament seriously. When the Royalist Army approached the town along the road from Tankersley, it found the way blocked by a barricade manned by thirty boys from the local grammar school. Accounts then differ. The Royalists claim that the town fell in one day, their opponents claim that it took at least two days to quell resistance. Whatever the case, some '1400 armes' were found, indicating that the town could have been well defended.

It seems likely, then, that the force advancing north towards the West Riding at Tankersley, were from Rotherham. No Parliamentary account of the action has yet been found, so we have only the two Royalist estimates of the number of troops as something like 2000–3000. Assuming at least some level of exaggeration for propaganda purposes, it would be reasonable to believe that the forces were relatively evenly matched in terms of numbers.

At Seacroft and Adwalton Moor manœuvring armies had met and clashed on the march across the terrain they happened to be in. Tankersley Moor, however, would seem to have been a more planned engagement. The Moor was a site well known to many on both sides and records show that it and neighbouring Harley Moor were used several times as training areas by local trained bands in the years leading up to the war.

The area itself sits in a shallow saddle between hilled country on both sides. It forms a gently sloping, but relatively even, expanse of land immediately to the south of what is now Junction 36 of the M1 motorway. Although much of the land adjacent has been drastically altered by the building of roads, a golf course and the encroachment of housing developments, there is still a large and relatively undisturbed area into which a battle of the scale suggested by the Duchess of Newcastle could fit.

According to an unpublished account of the battle held in the local library, 'the Royalist Army came on by Moor Lane'. The author does not give any provenance for this information, but it appears logical. If the Royalist Army were in Barnsley, they would advance via the village of Worsbrough to the Moor along what is now the A61 (the current route bypassing the village was established as a turnpike in 1840). It is worth noting that the A6135, which acts as a continuation south to Rotherham, is also known as Wakefield Road and this would be the most likely route for the advancing Parliamentary force. This is corroborated by accounts of the Royalist assault on Rotherham having advanced through Masbrough along this road. Both sides would therefore have marched parallel to the M1 on the eastern side.

The site of the moor has been identified by reference to local place names. A short path just north of the motorway junction is known as 'Moor Lane' and leads now to a footbridge across the motorway into Tankersley. This position was confirmed on an 1855 Ordnance Survey map, which identified 'Moor Lane' as continuing in the direction indicated by the footbridge, linking into the A61 route today. A couple of hundred metres away is a large hotel, now known as Tankersley Manor but in 1855 identified as 'Moor Farm'. The area south of Moor Lane is designated 'Tankersley Common' and it is safe to assume that this is the moor itself. Today, the common exists as a patch of land adjacent to the motorway junction.

Taking Moor Lane as our start line, the battlefield may be the area from here south towards Tankersley Lane where the cannonballs were discovered in 1917. These appear to have been fired by light guns which limited range would reach from here to Tankersley Lane. Wargamer Noel Williams suggests that the slight ridge made by Tinker Hill and the commanding site of St Peter's Church would make this a good defensive position – although this would shift the Parliamentary forces away from the road link with their rear. They would effectively have wooded hillsides to their rear and right flank and Royalists to their front and left flank.

Some sources place the fighting in and around Tankersley Hall but this seems unlikely since the hall stood in the midst of an established deer park. The park, owned by Lord Stafford, is recorded as being in existence by 1527 and a herd of deer remained in the park as late as 1850. Melvyn Jones described the creation of deer parks as:

> … enclosing an area of land with a fence to keep the deer and other game in, and predators (wolves) and poachers out. The fence was called the park pale and consisted of either cleft oak stakes, often set on a bank, or a stone wall. Tankersley Park, one of the longest surviving local medieval parks, was completely surrounded by a stone wall.

Whether the wall existed to that extent at the time of the battle is unclear but a map of 1720 shows it in place. Within the walls, the park consisted of dense woodland and plains with scattered trees, coppice and 'holly hags' – areas of holly bushes grown as winter fodder. The park would be a difficult place to manœuvre troops, so we can identify this as the southern boundary of our battlefield.

Shortly after the battle, Royalist troops took Rotherham. Days later, Sheffield Castle fell with minimal resistance. Tankersley Moor is described as having been a rout and it would appear that the news was enough to thoroughly demoralise the Parliamentary garrisons. Fairfax was to write that the loss of the garrisons 'much elated the enemy and cast down the spirits of the people of these parts ... The Earl of Newcastle's Army do now range over all the Southwest part of the Countrey, pillaging and cruelly using the well affected party'.

The capture of Sheffield Castle was of great value to the supply starved Royalists. It was to become a munitions factory, supplying weapons and ammunition to Pontefract for dispersal. The forge at Wortley was certainly part of this effort and cannonballs from the period have been unearthed there.

As well as opening the route south, the fight ensured that the Fairfaxes were alone and under pressure. It was to be a significant contribution to the eventual Royalist control of Yorkshire.

Set against the wider conflict, the campaign in south-west Yorkshire has been just a footnote to the story of the Civil Wars, but just because it is not famous does that make it uninteresting? What can an archaeological survey of Tankersley tell us? Tankersley was not a large or unusual battle. That is the key to its importance. It offers an opportunity to investigate a site that was selected by men who knew it as a training area. It is as if Salisbury Plain was to be the site of a major battle fought by men who had learned their craft there. Unfortunately, the owners of the land, mindful of the value of potential development and not wanting the inconvenience of a potential protected site, have refused permission for even the most basic fieldwork.

Nevertheless, the research demonstrates how it is possible, with minimal resources, to tie together the various strings of the story from easily available material. It also opens up other potential areas of investigation locally. To draw from the field of psychology, a battle is a gestalt entity. It is only understood as the sum of its parts and we need to look for patterns of thinking and behaviour that make up that sum. Peter Harrington has argued that more work 'needs to be focused upon the role of country houses in their role as garrisoned strongholds during the war' and Tankersley allows us to do just that. Sir Francis Wortley raised a garrison for two adjoining country houses and used them as bases from which to stamp his authority on the surrounding areas. The early days of the Civil War were as much about economics as military might and it was about gaining support for one side or the other. We need to look carefully at those who chose not to go to the ball and what that has to tell us about the real experience of the war.

History tends to tell us that Yorkshire was predominantly Royalist and, to an extent, this is true. However, as J.T. Cliffe has shown in his analysis of the Yorkshire gentry, this is not the whole story. In the West Riding of Yorkshire, the area that encompasses both the mill towns and the Rotherham/Sheffield region, he notes that 125 families declared for the king whilst only fifty-four were for Parliament. Significantly, though, 110 families remained neutral. The activities of Wortley and his men become important here in levying taxes but also in demonstrating to those neutralist families that Parliament could not protect them. It would be useful to see how this fear might have influenced the thirty-one families whose loyalties switched during the course of the war and the impact of this economic war on the local economy. By the time of the defeat of Fairfax at Adwalton Moor, he was to declare that West Yorkshire had been bled dry. Shortly after Tankersley we find Wortley issuing an order for the constables to raise soldiers. Recognising the difficulties, he tells them that rather than the 1000 men he has been asked for, he will settle for 500. A week later, an angry message was sent to them for their failure to deliver even that number.

The battle of Tankersley Moor was a small, forgotten episode in a bloody period of history. Finding the site is of no great significance in the context of the work being undertaken at Naseby or Edgehill, but it does add to the overall knowledge of the war and that alone makes the project worthwhile. Research into other sites of forgotten battles and skirmishes could help to develop a far greater understanding of the strategy and tactics of the time than we can gain from the setpiece battles that stand out in history because they were so very different from the experience of the majority of the population.

Not just a name on a wall: tracing individuals

Britain has always had an ambivalent attitude towards its soldiers. Wellington famously described the men under his command as the 'scum of the earth' and Kipling's famous poem about the common soldier 'Tommy' described the ambivalence of British society to its army, where as late as 1913 many pubs, theatres and music halls refused entry to soldiers as a matter of course. When one young man announced he wanted to join the army as a private, his mother said that she would 'rather see him dead than in a red coat'. Her embarrassment may have been eased as he rose through the ranks to eventually become a general, but the sentiment was widespread in 'respectable' British society. Unlike its European neighbours Britain did not use conscription widely and National Service has only been enforced for 26 of the army's 360-year history. Sociologists have written of 'economic conscription' to the forces brought about by poverty and unemployment, but enlistment was, and is, in the end a voluntary commitment. In Europe, Napoleon's conscript army drew recruits from all walks of life and service was seen in a more positive light, but in Britain, where the public had no obligation to serve, people were able to distance themselves from those who, for whatever reason, chose to join up.

A very clear class divide emerged. Napoleon believed that 'every soldier carries a Field-Marshall's baton in his knapsack' and that leadership should be granted on merit. As a result, the boundaries between social class and military rank in the French military were blurred to some degree. As fans of Bernard Cornwell's Sharpe novels and films will be aware, a British soldier could be commissioned from the ranks, but faced an uphill challenge. Even in the twentieth century, Richard Holmes has shown that a 1903 War Office Committee advised that an infantry officer should have at least £160 of private

38a, *b* and *c* Graffiti left by Australian troops in tunnels under Arras provide a snapshot of life on the Western Front

income per year in addition to his salary. As a comparison, the annual rent of a large family home in London at that time was around £100. Officers of the cavalry needed far more, around £600-700. The official salary for an officer at that time might be no more than £75 per year.

Earlier, we looked at the distinctions of 'us', 'people like us' and 'others'. Ordinary soldiers fell firmly into the latter category. Commissioned officers were acceptable in the 'people like us' category and it was considered a suitable occupation for those members of the gentry with nothing better to do. Ordinary soldiers were an expendable commodity with no particular value beyond their ability to use a weapon. Those killed in action would receive no special recognition but would instead be dumped in a communal mass grave once any useful items had been recycled. In the early nineteenth century, 'Waterloo teeth' enjoyed a measure of status among the better off. Teeth harvested from the dead of the battle were made into denture sets. The bones were often simply ground into fertiliser.

It was only in the twentieth century that soldiers began to receive recognition as members of society. In 1914, the British Expeditionary Force sent to France in response to the German invasion was a small but extremely professional army. The initial retreat took a heavy toll and the British government realised it would need to expand its manpower rapidly. Lord Kitchener led the creation of what became known as 'The New Army', drawn from towns and cities across the nation. In a wave of patriotic enthusiasm scores of thousands rushed to enlist. Whole factory shifts left work and marched themselves to recruiting depots. Sons, brothers, school friends and workmates joined up together with the promise that they would serve together in 'Pals' battalions. The local nature of these battalions was such that when heavy casualties began to be taken whole communities were plunged into mourning. It was not possible to repatriate the bodies of these citizen soldiers and so, across the country, local memorials began to spring up (see Neil Oliver's *Not Forgotten* (Hodder & Stoughton 2005) for an excellent account of this phenomenon).

The two World Wars have both been marked by the erection of local memorials honouring the dead and promising that 'their names liveth forevermore'. Unfortunately, the huge citizen armies of these wars created yet another divide in the way we remember our war dead. From the summer of 1968, the British military experienced a unique year in its history. No British service personnel were killed on active service. Since the end of what most people consider to be 'the last war', nearly 17,000 men and women have been killed in over 100 operations and campaigns around the world. In many cases, their families have been refused permission to have their names added to those of the dead of the two World Wars and, for many years, the annual Remembrance Service ceremonies referred only to those casualties and chose not to acknowledge the dead of other wars.

These distinctions in public attitudes towards the military are reflected in the information available to the researcher. Detailed records of First World War actions are relatively easy to find in a wide variety of formats. The Second World War is equally well covered with official and private papers in huge collections. Other wars are much less well represented. Part of the problem is, of course, a reflection of literacy rates and the ability of the common soldier to express himself but in every case, official records rarely name private soldiers – especially if they survived the action being described.

Tracing a service man or woman can therefore be a tricky business requiring a lot of luck. Those killed in action between 1914 and 1918, or 1939 and 1945, are given at least some official recognition through local memorials and rolls of honour and these are often a good starting point, as the example below demonstrates. Tracing a commissioned officer is a much easier prospect as they are much more likely to have been considered worthy of mention. Records of those who survived are much more difficult to access effectively.

All British soldiers have a personal file. Those prior to 1920 are held at the National Archive, those after that date remain with the Ministry of Defence and must be requested formally in writing. The First World War service record files are known as the 'burnt records' because the archive holding them was hit by bombs in the first German air raid on London on 7/8 September 1940 and many were either destroyed or damaged by fire and water. Of the First World War records in storage, about half were destroyed. Those records that survived were released to the National Archives at Kew in 1996 and can now be found on the catalogue database (www.nationalarchives.gov.uk). The original documents were so fragile that only microfilm is available for inspection and this requires a journey to the archives themselves. Whether an individual soldier's file survived is entirely random and so the researcher faces a potentially expensive and fruitless journey.

An alternative source for copies of these microfilms is the Church of the Latter Day Saints. The church has an enormous collection of files and records available on order through its family history centres around the country (www.familysearch.org). A keyword search of their library catalogue using 'burnt records' will lead you to the relevant files.

The British Army's divide between officers and men is evident, in that officers' files were stored separately and so had a higher survival rate. Around 216,000 were released to the National Archives in February 1998 relating to officers who served in the British Army between 1914 and 1920 and who had left the Army by 31 March 1922. It is often possible to locate an officer's file online by typing the surname into the National Archives Catalogue, accompanied with a record class number. Officers' files are mostly contained in record series WO 339 or WO 374 (especially Territorial officers).

Before starting any search, for any purpose, it is important to remember that the contents of both soldiers' and officers' personal files are unpredictable and can be greatly disappointing, but to approach research with the attitude that any information, however small, is a step forward.

One man's story: the death of George Galloway

George Galloway was a private soldier killed in the First World War. With just that piece of information, what can we discover about him and how he died?

If we are working backwards from a marked grave, its location will tell us something and we need to consider why it is where it is. If it is in the UK, then the man is almost certain to have died here. He may have been invalided home with a wound or disease that would eventually cause his death, or have been the victim of a training accident. If his grave is overseas, we need to look at the name of the cemetery. Many were built on or near the site of former dressing stations where the wounded would be gathered for triage to assess those likely to survive the further journey back to better equipped medical facilities. Two cemeteries in what was once the Ypres Salient, for instance, sound as though they are named for local Flemish villages, Dozinghem and Mendinghem, until you realise that they were, in fact, advance dressing stations (along with a third, Bandaginghem). If the grave is in one of these, then he is likely to have died of wounds having been brought back from the battlefield. If he has no grave but only a commemoration, he may have died on the battlefield and was either buried (perhaps by shellfire) or was not identifiable when recovered. 'May' is always the key term in these matters. Some soldiers were buried with all due reverence by their comrades only for the burial sites to be churned up later in the war by shellfire, destroying the graves.

In the 1920s, the Imperial War Graves Commission began the enormous task of ensuring that all the dead of the First World War had a lasting memorial of some kind. All identified bodies were buried in communal cemeteries marked by a headstone bearing their regimental badge, name, rank, number, age and date of death. Families could also have a personal inscription added to the base. Unidentified bodies were buried under a headstone bearing their regimental badge if it was known and a simple 'Known Unto God' inscription proposed by Rudyard Kipling, whose son Jack was among those whose remains were originally lost. Those who were not recovered, or who have no known grave, are listed on huge memorials, like those at the Menin Gate in Ypres or the Thiepval Monument on the Somme.

Today, the work of what is now the Commonwealth War Graves Commission (CWGC) continues with the annual recovery of yet more bodies from the killing fields of the Western Front. It continues to make efforts to identify the remains and to provide a dignified last resting place for all the war dead. Each burial or commemoration has been carefully catalogued as the 'Debt of Honour Register' and is now available online (www.cwgc.org). It is the most complete record to date of soldiers (and others) who died in the Great War and provides information on the exact location of the soldier's grave or his commemoration if he has no known grave. Apart from this, the information can be limited, as it was compiled from information supplied by relatives during and after the war. As a result the Register has a number of errors and there are projects working to rectify these. Despite its faults, the Register is the best place to start.

The site offers a search facility in which the surname and initials of a casualty, the force he served with and the approximate years of death are all used to produce a listing of possible candidates.

Many local authorities, schools and businesses created Rolls of Honour after the war and some are now available online. Others can be consulted at local libraries and town halls. It may be that these include additional information, such as the regiment or service number

Private Henry Clare
14/19, Cudworth

Private George Galloway
14/149, Barnsley

Private Archibald Hanson
14/636, Barnsley

39 George Galloway and his comrades, killed in a trench raid on 4 June 1916. *Jon Cooksey collection*

of the casualty, which will make it possible to identify the right person immediately. In this case, since we have neither, we need to examine all possible matches. Having completed the database search form, there are eleven recorded names matching 'Galloway, G':

1. GALLOWAY, GEORGE Service number 14/149. Died 04/06/1916
   A Private serving in the York and Lancaster Regiment. Aged 30 when he died and is commemorated on the THEIPVAL MEMORIAL, Face 14 A and 14 B

2. GALLOWAY, GEORGE Service number 13/1047. Died 01/07/1916
   A Private serving in the York and Lancaster Regiment. Aged 25 when he died and is commemorated on the THEIPVAL MEMORIAL, Face 14 A and 14 B

3. GALLOWAY, G Service number S/25634. Died 20/09/1918
   A Private serving in the Seaforth Highlanders. Age unknown. Buried at 1.VIS-EN-ARTOIS BRITISH CEMETERY, HAUCOURT

4. GALLOWAY, GEORGE Service number 1156. Died 29/10/1918
   A Gunner serving in the Machine Gun Corps (Motors). Age unknown. Commemorated Face 11. KIRKEE 1914-1918 MEMORIAL

5. GALLOWAY, GEORGE DAVID Service number 16802. Died 25/09/1915
   A Private serving in the Royal Scots. Aged 19 when he died and is commemorated on Panel 11.YPRES (MENIN GATE) MEMORIAL

6. GALLOWAY, DAVID Service number 12256. Died 17/07/1916
   A Private serving in the East Yorkshire Regiment. Age unknown. Buried: 315. 18. HULL (HEDON ROAD) CEMETERY

7. GALLOWAY, G H Service number 39065. Died 14/12/1917
   A Private serving in the York and Lancaster Regiment. Age unknown, buried VIII. C. 29. DUHALLOW A.D.S. CEMETERY

8. GALLOWAY, GEORGE I Service number 267233. Died 19/07/1916

    A Private serving in the Royal Warwickshire Regiment. Aged 22 when he died and is commemorated on Panel 22 to 25. LOOS MEMORIAL

9. GALLOWAY, G S M Died 04/07/1916

    A Second Lieutenant serving in The King's (Liverpool Regiment). Age unknown and buried O. 20. CAMBRIN CHURCHYARD EXTENSION

10. GALLOWAY, G T Service number 39152. Died 28/08/1918

    A Private serving in the Leicestershire Regiment. Age unknown and buried R. II. D. 15. ST. SEVER CEMETERY EXTENSION, ROUEN

11. GALLOWAY, GEORGE WOOD Service number 17630. Died 28/09/1918

    A Lance Corporal serving in the Royal Scots. Aged 23 when he died and is buried at G. 6. POTIJZE CHATEAU LAWN CEMETERY

We know that George was a private soldier so we can immediately discount GSM Galloway. We can also narrow down certain names for particular attention – we are looking for a Barnsley man and three names are listed for the York & Lancaster Regiment whose recruiting grounds included the Barnsley area. This process of elimination seems obvious but it needs to be used with care. In the early enthusiasm to join Kitchener's Army, men who found their local regiments full would often chose to enlist in whatever was available. Londoners joined Glaswegian units, Yorkshiremen appeared in Devonshire regiments. Later, as casualties mounted and conscription was introduced, the mix could be even greater.

Taking our three York & Lancaster (Y&L) soldiers, we have a number of options here depending on what we are looking for. If, for example, we are tracing George as a piece of family history we may want to know more about his life up to joining the army. We can see that there are three likely men aged thirty and twenty-five but the age of the third is unknown. Each would have been in work prior to joining the forces. By working out a birth year (1886 and 1891, respectively), we can use the freely available 1901 Census to find out more about the first two men and we can use the fact that the third has two initials to help refine a search for him. The Census will allow us to find out details about the man's background and family, even his address.

If we choose, we can go back to the 1891 Census (available online, but not free to use) to find out about their childhoods or we can go to the 1911 Census (not due to be digitised before 2012, but available at local libraries as a paper copy) to find out what they were doing just before the war. All were of working age so we should be able to discover their trades. This, too, may be useful later. There were 11 G. Galloways killed in the war but 51 who were eligible for campaign medals and we may need extra biographical information to distinguish each man.

On joining the army each man was issued a regimental number. Today, a service number stays with the recruit from enlistment to retirement, but in the First World War a man could be issued with a number for his training battalion, one for the battalion he first joins, another for each battalion he subsequently is posted to and yet another should he transfer to a new regiment or Corps. In this case, the biographical information will assist in identifying that 1104 Smith, P. who joined the Bloggshire Regiment in 1914 is the same Smith, P. who, by 1918, was serving as M403235 Smith, P. – a Driver in the Army Service Corps, transferred because of his pre-war training as a motor mechanic. The First World War Army was further confused by having, for a time at least, three distinct Armies – the small regular pre-war force that had led the BEF into France in 1914, the Territorial Force, reformed in 1908 for Home Defence and the New Army raised by Kitchener. The format of the service number issued to recruits could vary widely according to which of these forces he would eventually be posted. Having decided that in this case we are going to investigate 14/149 George Galloway, of the Y&L, we can use his number to identify that he served with the 14th Battalion (14/149). Another Galloway served with the 13th (13/1047) and another appears to have served in one of the other, probably regular, battalions. The low numbers indicate that these were early recruits to the new battalions, since service numbers are issued consecutively.

Using secondary sources drawn from a wide range of military history books available in the local library and First World War websites on the Internet, we can establish that the 13th and 14th Battalions of the Y&L were more often known simply as the 1st and 2nd Barnsley Pals respectively. From general histories of the war, we can establish that the Pals were formed in the patriotic fervour of 1914 and were posted to Egypt. They were then sent to France, arriving there early in 1916. Along with the regiment's 12th Battalion (Sheffield Pals) and the 11th Battalion of the East Lancashire Regiment (probably the best known unit of all the New Army – the Accrington Pals), the 13th and 14th Y&L formed the 94th Brigade of the 31st Division and were sent into the front lines near the village of Serre on what was then a relatively quiet sector – the Somme.

The CWGC database shows that George died on 4 June 1916, almost a month before the infamous first day of the Somme offensive. By trawling through 'Soldiers Died in the Great War' we can establish that he was one of six men of the Y&L to die on that date. Originally published in 1921, the compilations *Soldiers Died in the Great War* and *Officers Died in the Great War* were produced as a lasting memorial to the dead and widely published. Arranged by regiment or corps, *Soldiers Died* comprises a total of eighty volumes and the lists often give information that is not available in the CWGC Debt of Honour Register, such as the soldier's place of birth, residence, enlistment and any former regiment. Copies of the volumes covering local regiments are to be found in most of the larger public libraries and both works are now also available as a searchable CD-ROM published by the Naval & Military Press (www.naval-military-press.com). Although they are rather expensive for individual research, they are useful tools for researching unit histories. A cheaper alternative is available through the Internet, where it is now possible to search *Soldiers Died in the Great War* online (www.1837online.com). It is also possible to access the registers of war deaths.

We have a name, battalion and date for George's death. From this we can begin to make a more detailed search for specific information. Local newspapers almost always carried stories on local men killed in action, often with an obituary and sometimes a photograph. Copies of these are held in libraries on microfilm. George's death is in June of 1916, when the battalion was still very much an inexperienced unit with a strong local identity. A search of the public library reveals pictures of three men: George Galloway, Henry Clare and Archibald Hanson. All killed, according to the paper, during a trench raid on German lines on the night of the 3/4 June 1916.

Throughout the deadlock of trench warfare, the British general staff were keen to ensure that their men kept on the offensive. Such was the nature of the war that the Germans simply had to retain the land they had taken to claim victory. For the British, and more particularly their French Allies, victory could only come with the withdrawal of the Germans. As a result, the Germans dug deep and elaborate defences so they could sit tight. The Allies could never allow their men to adopt a similar attitude and so pressure was put on them to consider their trenches as only temporary measures. Night patrols and trench raids were used to hammer home the message that the Germans could never expect to be left alone. They were also an opportunity to gather information about the enemy's strengths and weaknesses and to acclimatise new units to combat gradually. With a large offensive looming, trench raids were a common feature of life on the Somme front.

Secondary sources can be used to gain an understanding of the tactics of trench raiding and there are many accounts in memoirs of the period. In the immediate post-war years, many regiments, and even towns, published souvenir accounts of the war years. Some are detailed records of actions involving specific battalions (especially those of the New Army), whilst others may simply be a compilation of local obituaries. An upsurge of interest in First World War studies has brought with it an ever growing list of titles about local regiments whilst many infantry regiments and battalions have published their own histories. Lists of some of these may be found through the catalogues of specialist booksellers, such as the Naval & Military Press (see above for website).

Some of these secondary sources may even have references to the actual raid itself, but it is in the hunt for primary source material, which could well provide a more detailed breakdown of the events surrounding the raid, that a rare pearl may be found. In this case a search of the local history archive of Barnsley library uncovered just such a nugget amongst a cache of original documents relating to the 14th Battalion in the First World War compiled from material sent or brought back from France by its officers. Among the actions described were extensive details of the planning for and after actions of the raid of 3/4 June. This was a lucky break, not all such documents deposited in or found their way back to local archives, but even if such a source could not be found locally, all units of battalion level and above were required to keep 'War Diaries' when on active service. These diaries are now preserved in the National Archives in record series WO 95. War Diaries rarely mention ordinary soldiers, but they do provide a detailed account of the unit's movements and activities on a given day. These are of varying quality, depending on who was writing them at the time and the circumstances under which they were being prepared – some are brief summaries of a day's activities, whilst others are detailed accounts of actions. Few are likely to mention soldiers by name but they will at least describe what the unit was doing on a certain day.

It is worth noting here, and is another reminder to cast one's research net wide, that several key documents which found their way back to Barnsley after the war to be deposited in the town library do not appear in the volumes of the 14th Battalion War Diaries at Kew. Their discovery thus enables a more detailed picture to be built up than the one which relied on the documents in the National Archives. In fact a typed and bound Battalion Roll of all those proceeding overseas with the 14th York and Lancaster Regiment was sent by its Commanding Officer Lieutenant Colonel William Hulke to the Town Clerk in Barnsley from their station at Hurdcott Camp near Salisbury, as the borough had borne the responsibility for raising, equipping and training the battalion until its formal adoption by the War Office. This roll proves beyond doubt that our soldier, 14/149 George Galloway, was a Barnsley Pal and further, that he attested on 13 January 1915 – one of 23 men who joined up that day – and gave his religion as Church of England. A fortunate find indeed.

It can also be a useful exercise to consult other sources in the National Archives to identify other units serving nearby at the time and use their records to fill in any gaps. They are available to study free at the National Archives themselves, or copies can be made. At present, a charge of £10 is made to provide an estimate of copying charges – once costs have been calculated, that £10 is deducted from the final amount. However, this can work out expensive. In one case, it cost £10 to obtain a copy of a four-lined letter dated 1946, stating that there was no information available! On the other hand, the information that might be contained in the file could answer every question. As with so much battlefield research, the only option is to target your request carefully and be specific about what it is you are looking for. Alternatively, for around £30 per hour, you can hire the services of professional researchers to find the papers for you – expensive, but not compared to the time, cost and energy involved in making a long journey. Using an Internet forum is a useful step at this stage. Sometimes you will find people who either already have the information and are willing to share it, or even offers from people living nearer the archives to look things up for you while they're there.

By April 1916, the Barnsley Pals had yet to face a real battle. They had served two tours of duty, opposite the ruined village of Serre where the trenches ran along four small copses, known to the men as 'Matthew', 'Mark', 'Luke' and 'John'. They had taken some casualties but were yet to undergo their trial by fire. In fact, they had only served a matter of days in the front lines and although confidence ran high, some must have wondered whether they were up to the job. It was decided that a large-scale raid should be launched to investigate the German trench system – at that point only 150yds from the British – to gather any information available about the German defenders and to give the men a chance to gain experience. Captain Alphonse Wood, A Company's commander, was to lead the raid, assisted by one of his platoon commanders, Lieutenant Harold Quest, and by a battalion scout, 2nd Lieutenant Best. Wood then selected nine NCOs and 12 men to operate two pairs of *Lewis* light machine guns to protect the raiding party's flanks. In all, 70 men would take part and each was allocated an identity number. George Galloway was number 19.

The plan called for artillery support, not only from 31st Division's guns, but from those of the neighbouring 29th and 48th Divisional artillery too. 60 guns, ranging from the standard eighteen-pounder field guns, right up to 9.2in siege howitzers, would be firing

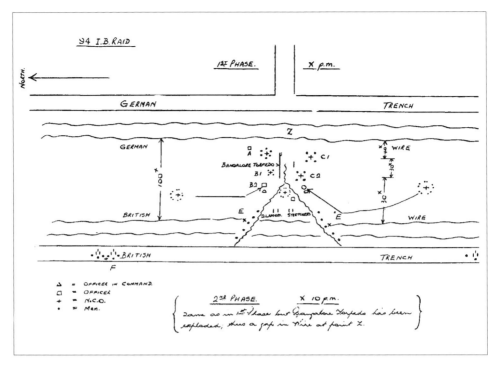

40 Captain Wood's plan for the attack. *Jon Cooksey collection*

to cover the raid. The start time would be 10 p.m. on 5 May. This was to be a large-scale operation by an standards.

The raiding party would use Bangalore Torpedoes (a 6ft long pipe filled with explosives and slid beneath the wire to cut a path), and with a major offensive in preparation, headquarters staff were keen to see how effective this might be. The barbed wire in this area was very thick and Lt Best experimented with varying lengths of torpedo until, by attaching several lengths together, he developed one 60ft long. This would surely clear a way for them. Over and over, Best and Lance Corporal Critchley practised putting the torpedoes together, knowing that on the night they would have to do it in the dark and exposed to fire. Each of the raiders rehearsed and rehearsed on practice trenches behind the lines.

The plan appeared straightforward. By 10 p.m. on the night of the 5 May, four small parties were to crawl through two gaps cut through their own wire and lie down in "no man's land". Two patrols would already have ensured that the area was free from German troops and would have laid a path of white tape across to the German wire to guide the raiders in and out. After the second patrol signaled that it was clear, an intense artillery barrage would begin, with shellfire forming a box which would prevent reinforcements reaching the area to be attacked. Lt Best would then blast the wire before a second barrage began. After an hour of bombardment, the raiding party would enter the

German trenches. Armed with revolvers, hand grenades, bayonets and clubs, three small groups of raiders would work their way along the fire and communications trenches to block any attempt to send troops to repel them. The main party would then attempt to cause as much damage as possible to the dugouts and machine gun positions. They would also take prisoners. The whole thing should take around 15 minutes.

By 2 May, everything was ready. The men were mentally and physically prepared and detailed orders sent out. Then, with just 24 hours to go, the operation was cancelled. The raiding party was consoled by hearing that it had been re-scheduled for 3/4 June, but if they had hoped for another month in which to hone their skills even further, they were disappointed. May was given over to training for 'the big push' that everyone knew would come soon. Training for the raid had to be fitted around the usual round of battalion training, fatigues, trench digging and rest periods. A final rehearsal at the end of May was watched by the Divisional Commander who congratulated the men on their preparations. On 2 June, British artillerymen began to lay their guns to the selected targets. The bombardment would be shorter than originally planned but even more guns would take part.

Just before dusk on 3 June, the raiders fell in outside A Company headquarters in Rob Roy Trench, just west of Matthew Copse. All badges, identity papers, paybooks and even personal letters were handed in. Nothing that identified a soldier could be taken. The aim was to gather intelligence, not to provide it. Faces were blackened and loose parts of uniforms tied back with string with strips of empty sandbags to act as camouflage. Pockets bulged with hand grenades and almost every man carried a hatchet or club.

The raid would go in at map reference 57DNE K29b1200 (see chapter four for an explanation of trench maps). This enables us to pinpoint the site today as being near the first of several small cemeteries on the track between the Serre Road and Sheffield

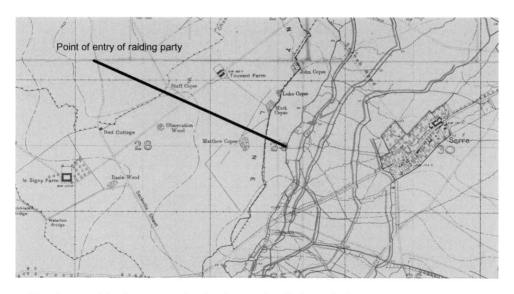

41 Trench map of the Serre sector dated early 1916. *Jon Cooksey collection*

Memorial Park, at 'Mark Copse'. The entry point into the German lines was directly opposite a section of trench held at that time by the 10th East Yorkshires, and the raiders picked their way with difficulty through the narrow trenches towards the start line.

Because we know that the trenches were held by the 10th East Yorks, we can use David Bilton's *The Trench: The Full Story of the 1st Hull Pals* (Leo Cooper 2002: 101–7) to get another perspective. Although the Hull men misidentified the raiders as being men of the Accrington Pals, Bilton's account leaves no doubt that it is the same incident. Private Pearson of the Hull Pals recalls 'that particular evening I stood at the gateway of headquarters and watched that party of raiders march past on their way to the line, with blackened faces and all the paraphernalia of trench warfare, singing and whistling and somehow I felt real sad for them'. (Bilton 2002: 103).

The crowded trenches delayed the raiders and it was almost midnight before they were in position. As the bombardment began, Lt Best and L/Cpl Critchley pieced together the lengths of the Bangalore Torpedo, and Privates Dunn and McKelvey began to drag it towards the wire. Suddenly, above the noise of the bombardment came a louder explosion and shell fragments sprayed down. McKelvey collapsed. Dunn carried the torpedo on and it was detonated as expected but, racing through the gap, he suddenly found himself facing 14ft of uncut barbed wire. Critchley came forward with wire cutters and spent five long minutes cutting through the vicious barbs.

The raid was in full swing, but before we go any further and find out what happened according to the British documentation, let us ask another question regarding sources. The Barnsley Pals were attacking German held trenches. This sounds like, and indeed is, stating the obvious, but if the British kept details of actions in War Diaries, perhaps the Germans did the same. Could there be, somewhere, in a German archive, a document that relates directlly to this action? If so can this offer another perspective, that from the 'other side of the wire'?

Again a search of the Internet and of secondary sources such as Chris McCarthy's *The Somme: The Day-By-Day Account* (Brockhampton Press 1998) makes it possible to identify which sector the Y&L were in. Consulting German books compiled just after the war or the several books which have, in recent years, focussed on providing a German perspective, will enable us to work out that the trenches which were the focal point of the raid were held by men of the German 169th Infantry Regiment of the 104th Infantry Brigade of the 52nd Division. This regiment had been formed during the late 1800s and by late 1897 had two battalions stationed in Karlsruhe and Rastatt. It was also known as the 8th Baden Regiment, its men being drawn from the Baden region of south-west Germany, in the valley of the Rhine, close to the frontiers of France and Switzerland. If documents could be located in Barnsley library, then perhaps a search of the local archives in the region from which the 169th Infantry Regiment sprang would bear fruit. And indeed detailed records and war diaries do exist, often written out beautifully in perfect script, with some even at the level of companies of the regiment.

Conducting a search for the dates 3/4 June 1916 reveals the gem required – a detailed after action report of the Pals' raid complete with the names and movements of those involved and with a diagram showing the layout of the trenches and the locations of the

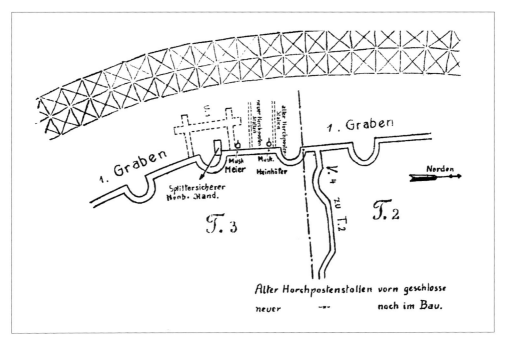

42 A German plan of the attack showing the positions of the sentries. *Jon Cooksey collection*

named men at the time the raid took place. Now we have a view of the same action from both sides and the primary documents even allow us to find out specific details for not only can we now discover the name and the movements of the German soldier wounded in the hand whilst taking cover in a tunnel but also the name of the man who shot him! With all these elements brought together, we can accurately record the events that led to the death of George Galloway.

And so we find that the British bombardment had alerted Major Berthold and Hauptmann Wetzke of the 169th Regiment and that they had called for their own artillery to fire on the British lines. In the front line, Oberleutenant Hodel, commanding 5th Company, consulted with Fahrich Arnold, one of his junior officers. The company had patrols in 'no man's land' that were now cut off by the bombardment and would only be able to get back in when the fire lifted. Then Arnold noticed the British bombardment switch from the fire trenches to the support trenches further back. Immediately he fired the red flares that would signal an urgent need for artillery fire to be directed on the British.

In the Hull trenches, the German fire began to impact within minutes. The Battalion History records:

> … hostile retaliation was prompt and heavy, and continued until 1.40, some twenty minutes
> after our guns had ceased, and every available German gun seemed to be firing on the short
> sector held by A and C companies. The front line trenches were blown in almost beyond

recognition, scarcely a fire bay remaining intact. As expected, casualties came rapidly, but the men stood up heroically to a rain of shells to which they could not reply'. Private Aust, experiencing his first barrage, later recalled that 'after about three minutes the German counter barrage came down and Bill Busby … and I spent most of our time being blown off the firestep and climbing up again (Bilton 2002: 103).

Only 150yds away, Critchley cut through the last strands of the wire and he was the first through, closely followed by Lts Best and Quest. They dashed for the trench line, already under fire. Musketier Heinhofer of 3rd Company 169th Regiment, on guard on the company's right flank, spotted the raiders and opened fire. At close range, L/Cpl Morgan opened fire with a revolver and hit Heinhofer in the hand. Heinhofer escaped down a disused tunnel, dug under the trench, which had once been used as a listening post.

By now, the carefully rehearsed plan had broken down completely. Instead of the fifty men detailed to take control of the trench, only a dozen, including George Galloway, had reached their objective and now frantically searched for anything remotely resembling the dugouts they had expected. A couple of possible holes were attacked with grenades but they could not locate a real target.

As the raiders tried to make sense of their position, Lt Best and L/Cpl Morgan were pursuing Heinhofer, firing their pistols down the tunnel after him. Heinhofer, now with a leg wound, screamed for help from his fellow sentry, Musketier Meier. Meier could not respond; he was unconscious in the entrance to a dugout some distance away. Emerging from a deep shelter, Musketier Meschenmoser could hear his comrade and rushed towards the raiders, hurling hand grenades at some men standing on the trench parapet.

By now, the Germans had recovered from the initial shock and a group followed Meschenmoser out of the deep dugout and began working their way down the trench using grenades and rifles, closing in on the Pals.

After just a few minutes, Captain Wood realised that the raid had gone wrong and that it would be futile to continue. He gave the password 'Kantara' as the signal to withdraw, and the message passed from raider to raider. Suddenly, a German grenade landed amongst a small group of the Pals. Lance Sergeant Garside was hit by six fragments, but beside him, George Galloway slumped to the ground, dead. As the raiders scrambled out of the trench and out into 'no man's land', his body had to be left behind. Dragging L/Sgt Garside with him, Private Symons was last out, throwing grenades behind him to delay the German pursuers.

Pausing only to collect wounded comrades as they went, the raiders rushed back to the British lines. By any standard, the raid had been a disaster. No dugouts had been destroyed, no prisoners taken and only two Germans had been wounded, Heinhofer and Meschenmoser, who had been hit by splinters from a grenade. Further north, one man had been killed and seven wounded by the British barrage. For the Pals, three men were dead, George Galloway, Henry Clare and Archibald Hanson, another fourteen wounded and Private McKelvey was missing. George Galloway and Henry Clare had joined up on the same day.

The retaliatory barrage continued for over an hour. Out in 'no man's land', the patrol Oberleutenant Hodel had been concerned about making their way back as soon as the firing eased. They had found what they thought were three dead Tommies and had recovered their weapons, but were unable to collect the bodies. They were left where they lay.

At dawn the next morning, a Hull sentry in the British lines saw movement 80yds out in 'no man's land'. A number of the Barnsley men were nearby, hoping to find out what had happened to their friends, when someone recognised the figure and without hesitation Private Clarkson climbed out of the trench in broad daylight and ran to help the wounded McKelvey. Seeing him struggle to carry his wounded colleague, Private Arthur Russell ran out to help. Together they brought him into the British trench, to the cheers of their comrades. Throughout, the Germans watched the rescue but despite the attack on them during the night, they held their fire. 'As the party regained our trench and the last man jumped down, a sniper fired a single shot over our bay in apparent admiration for a very brave though foolhardy exploit' (Bilton 2002: 106).

In the barrage that hit the British lines, 26 Hull Pals died, some buried alive as the trenches collapsed. About sixty were wounded. Three raiders were dead, another fourteen wounded. They had inflicted one dead and nine wounded on the enemy. Private Pearson, who had watched the raiders leave, learned later of the effects of the raid.

> It seemed the raiders had had a small success but with some casualties but the enemy retaliation had fallen upon our own people in the line and severe were the losses throughout the battalion. At least five of the lads who had joined around the same time I joined and had trained with me and lived in the same hut at Hornsea were killed and others seriously wounded … even though the raid went on record as a 'resounding success and the infliction of many casualties'. (Bilton 2002: 105-6).

Later that day, the Pals were relieved by the Bradford Pals and began the march back to the rest area of Warnimont Wood. As they passed their corps commander, General Hunter-Weston, he made a point of stopping the Y&L to congratulate them on their efforts the night before. With so many casualties, for so little result, the Pals were badly in need of the encouragement. Already the general staff had grave doubts about the ability of the New Army to fight independent small actions on its own initiative and the raid had simply reinforced that view. It had been decided that the coming offensive would work best if the Pals battalions were to advance slowly, as a group. This would ensure that progress was slower, but steadier, than allowing the men to run and so risk becoming dispersed. After all, the long bombardment would have destroyed the enemy machine gun posts and there would be no need to hurry.

The raid was recorded as a success. It was important for the morale of the tightly knit Pals battalions that they could believe that their friends had died for a reason and they would need to believe in their commanders. In four weeks, they would face their first battle, on 1 July. They would be 'going over the top' in the first wave.

In *Bringing Uncle Albert Home* (Sutton Publishing 2003), David Whithorn describes his own search for a relative killed on the Somme, and in doing so provides a model for this kind of research. Using similar methods, Alistair Fraser, of the 'no man's land' team of battlefield archaeologists, was able to trace the identity of a German skeleton from a broken and badly corroded identity disc, a few buttons and a glass pot lid (See *Battlefields Annual Review*, Pen and Sword Books 2005). The sheer size and scale of the war cemeteries of France and Flanders can make it impossible to remember that each headstone marks a real person.

George Galloway's body was never recovered. The roll of the 14th Battalion dead in Barnsley library reveals the initial burial sites of both Hanson and Clare – the Sucerie Military cemetery near Colincamps, where they lie still – who officiated at the burials and the date they were placed on the monthly grave return, but George Galloway's details are blank. He has no known grave and is remembered only as a name on a wall, but he lived and died as a human being. Singling out one grave or one name on a memorial to the missing and tracing the story behind it is a powerful and moving experience, even when, as here, the man is someone picked at random.

Conclusion

With careful research, we can not only identify how George Galloway died, but also where. By using primary and secondary sources, we can gather enough information to trace the route of the raiders and find the locations today. The chances that his body might be found are slim, to say the least. Even if it was possible, the lack of any identifying badges on the raiders' uniforms would make it impossible to say, with any certainty, whose remains they were. That is not the aim of this exercise. By using the same process, though, we can add a human element to the study of battlefields.

4

MAPS: FINDING YOUR
WAY AROUND

MAPS

It has frequently been said that the most dangerous threat to a soldier on any battlefield is that posed by an officer with a map. Used properly, maps are a useful tool, but they can also be a major source of confusion. Anecdotal evidence tells of monuments in surveys being counted twice simply because separate map references have been given by volunteers for the same site. In battlefield archaeology, where the location of artefacts within a possibly small area is of very real significance, the ability to understand and to produce accurate maps is a crucial skill. Maps are perhaps the most valuable, yet often the most mishandled tool available to the battlefield researcher.

This chapter will look at the basic skills necessary to use maps effectively. We will also look at the different types of maps available and how to use them before moving on to what is known as 'map regression' – using earlier maps, charts, written accounts and other geographical information to develop an understanding of how the physical landscape would have looked at the time of the battle. However, as useful as these maps can be as a means of orientating oneself to the battlefield, those guides in which troop deployments have been superimposed onto modern Ordnance Survey maps (e.g. Smurthwaite 1984) challenge even the most active archaeological imagination to fully appreciate how the Royalist cavalry coped with the one-way system or how Anglo-Saxon warriors were able to cross the car park under fire.

To begin with though, one of the first barriers facing the new researcher is that of understanding the information already available on a battlesite. Generations of military historians, often themselves former officers, have included in their accounts detailed campaign maps marked with the arcane symbols of little coloured boxes and arrows to chart the comings and goings of various units. These symbols are of enormous significance to understanding the unfolding action yet few writers have felt it necessary to include an explanation of the symbols, expecting instead a certain level of previous knowledge in the reader. Appendix B therefore gives a brief introduction to the use of military symbols. Those given are current NATO symbols and are widely used, although it is useful to remember that other armies, at other times, have used other conventions.

MAP TYPES

There are many different types of maps available to the researcher, some more useful than others and older maps, in particular, must be handled with care. Anthony Brown, for example, reports that there are three seventeenth-century plans of the Civil War defences of the main Royalist stronghold at Oxford held in the Bodleian Library. One of these has been printed with half of the layout upside down. Another, actually printed in a late seventeenth-century history of the University of Oxford, and accepted by some authorities as accurate, needs close inspection before it becomes apparent that it is too neat. It depicts a regular system of bastions set out mechanically around the city, taking no regard of the problems of the local terrain and the likelihood of flooding in the area. Oxford is, after all, a low-lying town. Only the third plan, with careful and accurate details and attributable to Sir Bernard de Gomme, a professional military engineer who probably helped to design them, can really be accepted as reliable (Brown 1987: 98).

Maps have been produced for a variety of political, practical and legal reasons over centuries to varying degrees of quality and can be accessed through local archives. These include:

Commercial maps

First appearing during the Tudor period, these often accompanied trade directories and mapped individual parishes, towns, cities and counties. Although crude by modern standards, these do at least enable us to identify road systems, river courses and built-up areas.

Estate maps

Landowners sometimes hired surveyors to map their possessions and these maps can help to clarify land use, field names and other clues. Such maps are the property of the landowners but may be available through family deposits to local archives.

Maps deposited at Quarter Sessions

Between the mid-eighteenth and mid-nineteenth centuries a series of localised Enclosure Acts were passed leading to the General Enclosure Act of 1845. In these maps, individual fields within a locality are charted and named. These can often provide useful clues since field names often derived from previous use of the land. For example, in the Cotswolds, the common field name 'Chessells', has been shown to be derived from an Old English word for 'a heap of stones' and frequently have indicated the site of a Roman villa (see other examples provided by Gilling 1984 or Whynne-Hammond 1992). Often, these field names are more obviously linked, such as 'Bloody Field' near Ackworth in Yorkshire which takes its name from the Civil War skirmish fought there or, of course, Towton's infamous 'Bloody Meadow'.

Later, applications for authorities to build turnpikes, railways and canals all had to be accompanied by the production of a map lodged at Quarter Sessions before Parliament could be approached for permission. All the Quarter Session maps are kept by the House of Lords Record Office.

of a decimal point) and may add Z (altitude), such as 300m. Used in the same way as the OS references, this should be accurate to 100m. The use of this grid system is made more difficult by the fact that the full grid is only drawn on some local maps and not others. Oddly enough, the system isn't widely understood, even in France, and may explain an awful lot about the French experience of war.

Trench maps

During the First World War, detailed maps were produced of enemy trench systems based on aerial reconnaissance photos. These mass-produced maps are available today through specialist militaria sources and from Internet sales sites. Members of the Western Front Association (see addresses) are able to access the association's extensive collection of maps, and the Imperial War Museum has produced a CD-ROM of maps covering the entire Western Front. All are invaluable for an understanding of any trip to the battlefields of the First World War. The maps were produced by overlaying a grid system onto the existing French maps, a complicated procedure that required an entirely new referencing system to be developed. A detailed explanation has been provided by Howard Anderson (2004) for the Western Front Association's website (www.westernfrontassociation.com) and also by Richard Holmes (2004: 453-5), but briefly, a First World War map reference consists of a series of letters and numbers. Each 1:40,000-scale map was divided into 6,000 yard squares, marked by a capital letter. These were subdivided into thirty-six 1,000 yard squares, each of these quartered into sub-squares, marked 'a-d'. Within these squares, a two or four figure grid reference could be determined. So, a First World War grid reference might be 51bNW3 G24b34. The whole of France and Belgium was mapped in this way so '51' gives a general area. Within this, '51b' narrows the search down to a sheet. Within this sheet, four more divisions split the map into NW, N, SW and SE. Each of these are further split into squares, marked '1-4'. So, in our example, '51' lies in northern France; '51b' covers the area around and east of Arras. The area '51bNW' covers the town itself, as well as the land north, north-east and east of it. The reference '51bNW3' is the 1:10,000 sheet showing Arras itself. On sheet '51bNW3', a capital letter, in this case 'G', denotes a 6000 yard square, and '24' indicates a 1,000 yard square. Within this, 'b' indicates the top right of four boxes within that square. Dividing that box up into ten smaller squares, numbering from the south-west corner along the bottom of the square, then around where '3' would be, we mentally draw a line up the box. Now repeating the same exercise up the side of the box, another line around where '4' would be, goes across the box. Hopefully, where the two cross, we should find two dugouts on Gloucester Terrace trench, halfway between the village of Blangy and Fred's Wood. Simple really – considering they are based on French maps.

Air photography

Alongside maps, aerial photography can be an extremely useful tool in identifying earthworks and defensive structures. Such photographs are accessible through Internet sites and should be consulted to complement the use of maps. Unfortunately, though, for the most part these are not taken by or for archaeologists. Pictures taken when the sun is low in the sky, or when frost helps define contours, are more likely to show up as sites but those taken with this in mind are harder to come by. The art of photo interpretation is just that, an art, and it is easy to mistake blurry blobs on a black and white picture for something completely different, so care must be taken when using these pictures. Having said that, if you are able to find them then they have the potential to add significantly to the map exercise, especially for anyone investigating twentieth-century warfare where contemporary aerial shots may be accessible.

Site plans

Archaeological records frequently include a map of the site to show the layout of trenches and features. These are generally self explanatory but the system of indicating earthworks can be confusing at first. These are indicated by the use of tadpole-like symbols known as 'hachures'. These consist of a dot to indicate the top of the feature with a tail, the length of which indicates the size of the feature. So, where the dots meet in two lines, the feature is raised (a wall or embankment); where the tails meet, it is a ditch or moat.

Land, as we have seen, is in constant use. Roads and towns are built, rebuilt and expanded time and time again; woods are cleared and others planted; rivers are dammed or they shift course and, when the military have moved on, farmers return the land to the plough. The maps we use provide us with an accurate representation of the ground today but we really need to know what the land was like at the time, if we are to understand the decisions that were made. To do this, we need to conduct what is known as a 'map regression' exercise to develop a map of the area at the time we are interested in. A useful starting point for an exercise like this is the local A-Z directory of streets. Often, these can provide clues to long lost locations through street and place names.

Throughout the country, place names frequently reflect military connections. Roman fortifications, for example, are often remembered in 'chester' or 'caster' suffixes, whilst 'bury', 'brough' and 'borough' can be linked to Anglo-Saxon 'burghs' or fortified townships (Jones 2000). Elsewhere, 'Bloody Meadow' at Towton refers to the field in which so many Lancastrians lost their lives as their army was routed. Moor Lane at Marston Moor is still known locally as 'Bloody Lane', and local children dare one another to walk along it at night (Cooke 2004: 187). Tankersley Moor, site of a 1643 battle, has disappeared from the map, remembered now only by 'Moor Lane', a short residential street alongside the M1 motorway. These clues help to define our search area and make it easier to compare an area over time. Taking this last action as an example, the action is known only from one reference to it by that name in the biography of the Duke of Newcastle, written shortly after the event. Although Tankersley Common remains on the OS map, it is an area that has been subject to opencast mining and sits on the eastern side of the motorway. By referring to maps produced before the building of the motorway, we find that Moor Lane once extended much further than it does today. In fact, from the mid-nineteenth century OS map available on the Internet, we find that Moor Lane once followed the route of what is now the A61 on the western side of the M1. More than that, we find that the large hotel on the A61 was, in fact, known until fairly recently

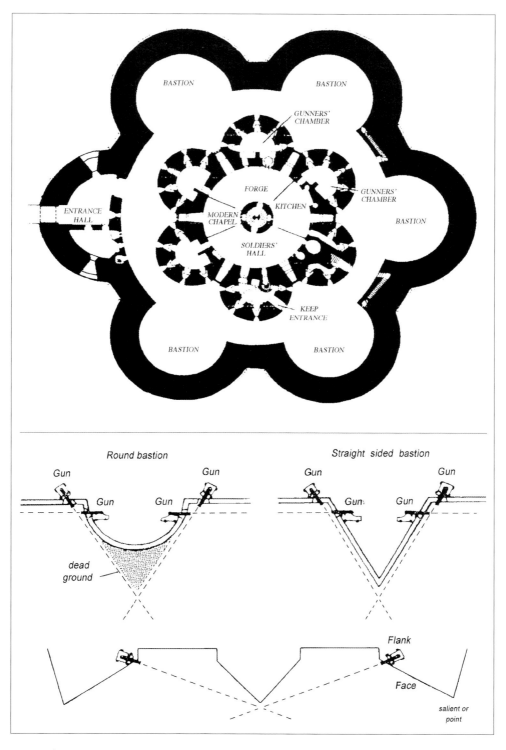

45 Fortification plans showing different types of design. Planel, 1995

as Moor Farm. Very quickly, the likely boundaries of a search area have been defined and are some distance from where it would seem to be indicated. A quick trip to the local library turns up an enclosure map with Moor field clearly marked near Moor Lane, not far from Moor Farm. These are the kind of clues that can significantly shift a search area away from accepted sites and towards where the evidence may actually be.

David Johnson, whose 2003 study of the battle of Adwalton Moor provides an excellent case study in how map regression can be used to recreate the seventeenth-century landscape, writes of the general method by which this is achieved. Three types of evidence need to be brought together: historic documentation, an interpretation of the physical landscape, and archaeological investigation. The process begins with gathering together all available references to the area at the time – maps of any kind, land title records, business accounts and eyewitness descriptions of the action. Each of these adds another piece to the jigsaw. Business accounts, for example, may tell us about some form of industry in the area – the use of 'bell pits' to extract minerals will automatically affect the deployment of troops and the use of cavalry, and heavily ploughed fields will also hamper movements. These factors need to be added to the equation in order to better understand what commanders saw on the ground at the time. This is then followed by a landscape interpretation exercise in which the written sources are compared to the ground in order to determine the extent of the site – the method used by English Heritage in developing its battlefield register. This involves walking the site to identify existing features that are contemporary with the action – a church, a river, a road – that will act as a landmark to orientate modern and reconstructed maps. Finally, the recovery of artefacts is used to further interpret the site. Although the scientific recovery of artefacts is of course the aim, local records frequently refer to finds made by workers over the years during ploughing or clearance, all of which help to further confirm a location.

Following Johnson's model, we can look firstly at the modern map and use it to establish a number of features for further investigation:

High ground

Control of the high ground is an important tactical advantage in any form of action. It allows a commander a better view of the surrounding area and forces attackers to both fight and climb, making it a useful position to seize and hold. As a result, these are the positions likely to feature in accounts of the fighting. Problems arise where the actual names of these features are unknown or disputed. At Adwalton, Johnson needed to determine whether 'Wiskit Hill', 'Wisked-hill' and the modern Westgate Hill are the same feature. The use of modern topographic maps enables the researcher to identify high ground by interpreting the contours. By transferring the contours onto a plain sheet, the actual shape of the land can be recreated. This provides the foundation for us to begin to populate the model with other relevant features.

Roads, lanes, villages and buildings

The Roman occupation of Britain left the country a lasting legacy in the form of a network of roads connecting the major population centres. In continual use for two

47a and *b* Battle damage from fighting in May 1940 evident on the First World War Indian War Memorial near Neuve Chappelle

film user, and you have moved a step closer to understanding the lay of the land from a military perspective.

Conversely, the more modern the action, the lower the perspective. In trench warfare, for example, we need to remember that the land was seen from below ground level through trench periscopes. In the Second World War, the average infantryman is unlikely to have seen much of the action above 18in from the ground if he planned to survive it. Hence, when we visit sites, we need to remember that the obvious approach route to us may not have been obvious at the time. More than one memorial has been sited where military logic states an incident should have happened rather than where it actually did.

Battle damage

For centuries, fortifications were assaulted by various means. Some of these have left their marks. At Pontefract Castle the tunnels dug by sappers intent on undermining the walls can still be seen. At York repairs to the walls from a more successful attempt can be seen at St Mary's Tower near the Minster. Elsewhere, other, more obvious evidence of attack is found around actions involving explosives and firearms.

Throughout major cities in the UK, older buildings may bear the scars of bomb damage. Once the tell-tale marks of 'bomb spatter' have been recognised, they become obvious clues to the sites of bomb attacks. Fans of forensic detective television shows will be familiar with the concept of blood spatter and how this can be traced back to the point of origin by the size and shape of the droplets. Bomb fragments behave in much the same way, leaving tear-shaped gouges with the narrow end towards the point of the explosion. Small-arms fire tends to be more direct and so the impact of rounds leaves a 'dent'. Again, the size and shape can give some indication of the size of the weapon and its firing point.

In softer ground, only larger explosions leave a recognisable trace, although the battlefields of the Falklands still bear the marks of mortar fire which has burnt and killed the slow growing grasses, leaving them as patches of bare earth even twenty-five years later. For the most part, though, bomb and shell craters have been eradicated by ploughing. Where they remain, their tear shaped profiles provide obvious evidence of the direction of fire. Bombs, by definition, are dropped from above and tend to create a more circular crater, as anyone who has flown over the fields of North Vietnam will know. Huge rows of round ponds today mark the paths of B52 bomber strikes across the country. Similarly, mines exploded under the trenches of the Western Front have left similar rounded craters, such as that at Lochnagar on the Somme.

Trenches

Military trenches are dug to very clear plans. Soil is taken out of the trench and placed to the sides to form a barrier to incoming small arms fire on the side facing the enemy (the parapet) and another barrier to protect from artillery fire or attack from behind (the parados). Often, a trench system will be deliberately filled in by the troops themselves, shoveling the loose soil back into the trench. This then settles over time but will often

48 Evidence of shellfire. These tear-shaped craters on the *Pointe du Hoc* provide a clear indication of the direction of fire (from behind the camera)

Left and below: 49a and *b* Artefacts:
Blowpipe missile case, Falklands (a);
First World War dugout roof, now
compost heap (b)

Right and below: 50a and *b* The Iron
Harvest. Shells collected during
ploughing await collection by the army

51 Hedges are a particularly fertile area for searching. Here a First World War wire support still holds barbed wire after 90 years

1 Landscapes of war: a derelict Churchill stands at the entrance to an industrial estate in South Yorkshire, the sole reminder of the contribution of local armaments workers to the Second World War

2 An Argentine sangar on the western approach to Mount Longdon, Falkland Islands

Right: 3 Now a memorial park, the *Pointe du Hoc* is also an official war grave for the German and American troops whose bodies still lie somewhere under the rubble

Below: 4 Landscapes over time: Chinese Cham towers and French and American bunkers record a history of occupation at a strategic point on Highway One, Vietnam

5 'A multimodal landscape of remembrance'. On the Somme battlefield, a sign advertises local services

6 Memorial crosses for each of the British paratroopers killed on Mount Longdon, Falkland Islands

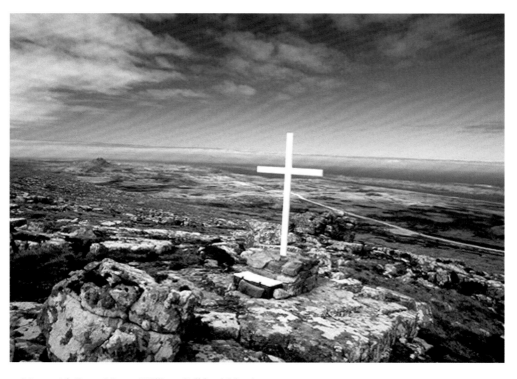

7 Memorial Cross, Mount William, Falkland Islands

8 'Two years in the making, ten minutes in the destroying'. A cross marks part of the field in which the Accrington Pals lost 585 men in a matter of minutes on 1 July 1916

15 Another slit trench. This time part of the perimeter established by 'the lost battalion' on Hill 314 during the German counter-attack at Mortain

16 Argentine boot, Falkland Islands

Above: 17 Granville, France. In the old town, a British cannonball remains where it landed in the eighteenth century

Right: 18 A military truck rusting quietly alongside the 'Redball Express' supply route through Normandy

19 Warning signs at Vimy Ridge, France

20 The Iron Harvest. These sorts of items still litter the fields of France and Belgium and still claim lives

21 This concrete bunker, now almost overgrown, stands in the main street of the village of Festubert, France. From 1918 to the late 1970s it was used as a family home

22 Experimental archaeology: no better way to understand why soldiers behave as they do

23 Experimental archaeology: a First World War gun group on the move

24 Experimental archaeology: recreating an American Civil War battlefield and its aftermath

leave a slightly lower area where the loose soil in the trench compacts down and settles below the original ground level. A regular shaped indentation easily identifies where this has happened.

Alternatively, where a trench system is not filled in, the soil from the parapet and the parados is gradually washed into the hole by rainfall creating a 'V' shaped ditch. Military trenches are never dug in straight lines as this would simply channel explosive power down their length, causing greater casualties. Instead, trenches are dug as zig-zags or as a series of bays that look from above like the battlements of a castle. These help to minimise the damage caused by explosions and provide greater fields of fire for defenders. As a result, any 'V' shaped ditches not running in a straight line along a field boundary are worth investigating.

Artefacts

Even before beginning a search, artefacts may be apparent. The more remote the battlefield, the more likely it is that evidence will remain on the surface. In France, the annual 'iron harvest' is still evident at the edges of recently ploughed fields. At Arromanches and Utah Beach in Normandy, the remains of the massive Mulberry floating harbours are just two of the thousands of structures still in place.

Recycled material

Modern warfare creates a need for massive amounts of equipment. Much of this is salvaged by the forces themselves after the action has moved on but not everything can be taken away. In the UK's bomber counties, airfields now house business parks and machinery but the origin of the buildings is obvious. Every battlesite, in any age, is a potential goldmine for the local civilian population. Everything from food and clothing to vehicles and even homes can be grabbed by the opportunist. Atlantic Wall bunkers now act as homes or garages for French families. The steel mesh strips used to build landing strips for Allied fighters now line the hedges of fields across Normandy. Junk shops abound with US, British and German cast offs and any corner of a field can turn up unexpected reminders of the passage of war.

The aim of map-based research is to narrow down the search area to a general area. Walking the area then further defines the search area by eliminating those sections of the field where further searching would be impractical and highlighting those likely to yield results. It also serves to put the site in its wider context by allowing an explanation of the approach routes, the likely start line and the route of an advance to contact by opposing forces. Done properly, it should provide enough evidence for a likely battlesite to be identified, ready for a more detailed survey.

5

ARCHAEOLOGY AND THE LAW

Once a target area has been identified by desktop research, a decision needs to be taken about what further evidence is needed and how it might be found. In the case of a battlefield, the obvious evidence will come from the presence and location of spent munitions and other military debris across the landscape. Tim Sutherland has written that 'the most important archaeological layer on a field of battle is the topsoil' (2004: 15). It is in this top layer that most of these artefacts are likely to be found. This makes it possible to conduct battlefield archaeology without the need for expensive equipment but unfortunately this in itself can be a problem. Since it is so easily accessible, it is attractive to those with other motives – hence the large number of battlefield relics turning up on Internet sales sites and militaria fairs. It cannot be emphasised enough that once an item is removed from the ground, most of what it has to tell us is lost unless it is properly recovered.

Serious consideration needs to be given as to whether the resources are available to you in order to achieve safe recovery of artefacts before plans can be put in place – especially on twentieth-century sites, where the possibility of uncovering extremely dangerous explosive and chemical weapons remains an altogether real risk. If potentially dangerous materials are likely to be found, what measures are you able to take to ensure site safety? Military bomb disposal or, more accurately, Explosive Ordnance Device (EOD) teams based around the country are able to offer advice and would be needed to make safe any live ammunition you may find. Generally, their advice is to stay well away from it and don't go looking – after all, if it doesn't kill you, it may kill them. Remember that these people have a serious and important job to do, so it is important that you show them the courtesy of having good reason to take up their time. In Belgium, for example, the *Dienst voor opruiming en vernietiging van ontploffingstuigen* (DOVO or Service for the Disposal and Demolition of Explosives) maintains a fulltime presence in Flanders to deal with the thousands of tons of explosives still lying in fields throughout the region. It is said that at a rate of five gas shells made safe per day, there is still a 30-year stockpile awaiting attention. Clearly, they will prioritise and provide training to those teams showing a serious and legitimate intent, but cannot support souvenir hunters.

Further consideration needs to be given to the actual aim of the survey. If you are searching for evidence of a Civil War battle, what are you going to do with the Roman

52 Signs around the Canadian Memorial at Vimy Ridge graphically show why unauthorised metal detecting is discouraged along the lines of the Western Front

sword that turns up? As Sutherland (2005) has said, it is important to think in terms of a battlefield project that allows for, and anticipates, military use of an area over time. All finds will need to be recorded, whether they fit into the period expected or not, and will also need identifying and preserving. The Portable Antiquities Scheme (PAS) is a network of archaeology professionals around the country acting as a point of contact for members of the public and should be approached for advice. It may be possible to liaise with them and have someone on site to assist and advise.

In addition to these considerations, careful thought also needs to be given to the legal issues around conducting any sort of ground search. What follows is a brief guide to relevant legislation but the situation is rapidly changing, especially in relation to battlefield relics. You are advised to check the current situation carefully.

The Protection of Military Remains Act 1986 was brought into force by an Act of Parliament in the UK to provide protection for the wreckage of military aircraft and designated military shipwrecks. There are two types of protection under the Act: Protected Places and Controlled Sites.

PROTECTED PLACES

The main aim of designating a site as a protected place is to protect the last resting place of service personnel as officially recognised war graves.

All crash sites of military aircraft are automatically designated Protected Places, irrespective of how the crash happened, whether there was loss of life or whether it took place in wartime. Therefore, any wreckage of a military aircraft is officially a protected place, even if the physical remains have not been previously discovered or identified. There have been prosecutions of aviation groups for disturbing a crash site, even with the permission and support of the next-of-kin of the pilot.

Shipwrecks are designated by the name of the ship and can be designated as protected places even if the location of the site is not known, providing the ship sank after 14 August 1914. The designation does not only apply to naval vessels following a ruling in the High Court known as the 'The Storaa Judgement'. The SS *Storaa* was a merchant vessel sunk by a German torpedo on 3 November 1943 whilst sailing as part of a military convoy. The crew included both Royal Navy personnel and merchant seamen.

In 2005, the daughters of one of those killed on the *Storaa*, Rosemary Fogg and Valerie Ledgard, launched a judicial appeal against the Ministry of Defence's decision to refuse to designate the wreck. In the High Court, it was decided that the ship could be designated. The Ministry of Defence appealed the decision and the matter went to the Appeal Court, which upheld the decision that the Act could apply to merchant vessels sailing under military command. This does not mean that all such ships will be designated, but that they can be.

Although the Act makes it an offence to interfere with a protected place, divers may visit the site but are advised to 'look, don't touch and don't penetrate'. It is an offence to disturb or to remove anything from the site and the law technically applies anywhere in the world; although, in practice, outside the UK, the sanctions can only be enforced against British citizens or ships, unless backed by local legislation.

CONTROLLED SITES

Controlled sites must be specifically designated by location and apply to sites containing the remains of a vessel sunk within the last 200 years. The act makes it illegal to conduct any operations, such as diving, that might disturb the remains, unless specifically licensed by the Ministry of Defence to do so. Since the Ministry of Defence has its own diving teams that are capable of carrying out any diving operations considered strictly necessary, it is highly unlikely that a request for such a license would be granted. Controlled sites are marked on admiralty charts and their physical location is marked by means of a buoy.

By 2006, there were fourteen controlled sites and six designated protected places (five British wrecks in international waters and one German U-boat in UK waters). The 90th Anniversary of the Battle of Jutland, on 31 May 2006, was marked with an announcement that the remains of the fourteen British ships lost in that battle were being designated as protected places.

The National Council for Metal Detecting (www.ncmd.co.uk), the governing body for the metal-detecting hobby, is keen to develop the use of metal detecting within

53 This quiet field was once a killing ground but only the cross hints at its dark history

mainstream archaeology and has published international legal requirements on its site. You should check this carefully for updates. Briefly, however, the situation is this:

England and Wales

There have been a number of Acts passed into law for the protection of sites of historical significance, including the Ancient Monuments and Archaeological Areas Act (1979) and the National Heritage Act (1983), but these have been largely ineffective. Grant *et al.* (2002) claim that only 2 per cent of known sites have so far been listed and argue that these laws have often been overlooked by landowners who claim ignorance or local authorities who do not prioritise heritage concerns. They also point out that these Acts don't apply to landscapes. Before undertaking any survey, the local Sites and Monuments Record (see contacts and resources section) should be consulted to check the status of your site.

The main legislation affecting the type of field survey we are discussing is the Treasure Act (1996), which covers all finds made in England and Wales. The British Museum's guidance (www.finds.org.uk) declares that the following are defined as 'treasure' if they were found after 24 September 1997 (or, in the case of category '2', if found after 1 January 2003):

1 Any metallic object, other than a coin, that comprises at least 10 per cent precious metal (i.e. gold or silver) by weight and that it is at least 300 years old when found. It will be regarded as treasure if any part of it is precious metal if it is of prehistoric date.
2 Any 'group' (i.e. two or more metallic objects) of any kind that appear to be of prehistoric date that come from the same find (see below).
3 All groups of coins found together provided they are at least 300 years old when they are found (although if the coins contain less than 10 per cent of gold or silver there must be at least ten of them). Only the following groups of coins will normally be regarded as coming from the same find:
    • hoards that have been deliberately hidden.
    • smaller groups of coins, such as the contents of purses, that may been dropped or lost.
    • votive or ritual deposits.
4 Any object, whatever it is made of, that is found in the same place as, or had previously been together with, an object that is considered to be treasure.
5 Any object that would previously have been treasure trove, but does not fall within the specific categories given above. Only objects that are less than 300 years old, that are made substantially of gold or silver, that have been deliberately hidden with the intention of recovery and whose owners or heirs are unknown will come into this category.

All such finds should be notified to the local coroner within fourteen days of the find. The coroner can be contacted via the police or the Portable Anitiquities Scheme.

Wrecks

The Treasure Act and the Portable Antiquities Scheme apply to objects found on land. Any object recovered from the sea either directly or washed ashore on the beach, or from tidal water is referred to as 'wreck'. All items, regardless of what they are, brought out of the sea must be reported to the Receiver of Wrecks at:

The Receiver of Wreck
Bay 1/05, Spring Place
105 Commercial Road
Southampton
SO15 1EG
www.mcagency.org

Scotland

The situation in Scotland is different. The National Museums of Scotland Treasure Trove Advisory Panel has issued guidelines for fieldworkers (www.treasuretrove.org.uk). This states that under the *regalia minora* common law rights of the Crown in Scotland, it is the prerogative of the Crown to receive all lost and abandoned property.

There is a narrow definition of 'treasure trove' per se, involving precious items which have 'lain concealed', but in practice this is overridden by the wider legal concept of *bona vacantia* (or 'ownerless goods'). The crucial maxim within Scots common law is *quod nullius est fit domini regis* ('that which belongs to nobody becomes our Lord the King's [or Queen's]'). Thus all objects whose original owner or rightful heir cannot be identified or traced are automatically considered to be the property of the Crown. Unlike English law, it does not matter whether objects were lost or intentionally hidden, or what material the objects are made of. The Crown Office in Scotland has the duty, overseen by the Scottish Executive, to claim *bona vacantia* on behalf of the nation.

Operation of the Treasure Trove system

The Treasure Act 1996 in England and Wales does not apply in Scotland, but the system by which archaeological objects are dealt with under *bona vacantia* is also known in Scotland as 'treasure trove', though it is important to distinguish this from the Treasure Act. In order to exercise its rights over archaeological finds under *bona vacantia*, the Crown Office relies on the recommendations of an expert group known as the Treasure Trove Advisory Panel, made up of Members of the Panel, who serve voluntarily. The Panel has an independent chairperson and four members drawn from the museum and wider heritage community who do not represent any special interest groups and are appointed by the Scottish Ministers on the basis of their expertise and experience.

Should I report everything I find?

As anywhere else, probably the majority of items found in Scotland, whether casually or by using metal detectors, will not be of any real archaeological or historical significance. Items, such as pieces of broken farm machinery, twentieth-century coins, washers, nails and other recent everyday objects, will not be claimed and need not be reported. However, you should be aware that the Treasure Trove law applies to finds of both precious and non-precious metals, all coins, and also any non-metal antiquities, including pottery, stone axe heads and objects of flint, wood, glass, leather and bone.

What types of finds will be returned to me?

Coins

Coins will be taken for identification and, in the case of pre-1707 coins, recorded in the Scottish Coin Register. In most cases, coins will be returned to the finder along with identification details.

Other finds

In many cases, finders may be able to judge the significance of finds and whether they need to be reported. If there is any doubt about identifying an object, though, it is better to be safe than sorry and report all potentially significant finds. Normally, any finds not being claimed will be sent back to the finder, unless these are heavy or fragile. In such cases, the TTAPS will discuss return arrangements with the finder.

What kind of finds are claimed?

Usually, only finds of archaeological and historical significance will be claimed by the Crown. These can include some relatively common types of objects such as lead seals, buckles, and brooches, which are sometimes claimed if they contribute new information. Other objects may be claimed because they come from locations which have previously yielded significant finds and help to build a picture of past activity in that area.

Northern Ireland

The use of metal detectors in Northern Ireland is covered by the Historic Monuments Act (NI) 1971 which states:

> Part IV Section 11: A person shall not, save under and in accordance with a licence … dig or excavate in or under any land … for the purpose of searching generally for archaeological objects …
> Part IV Section 12: The finder of any archaeological object … shall, within fourteen days of such finding, report the circumstances … to the Director of the Ulster Museum … or to the officer in charge of a police station

Jersey and the Channel Islands

The naval history and German occupation of the Channel Islands has left a great many sites of potential interest. Jersey has no comparable legislation to the mainland Treasure Trove acts, but there are issues to consider:

1   Parks and Common Land areas are out of bounds to metal detectorists.
2   SSI – Sites of Special Interest. These cover all historic sites and buildings in Jersey,

and detecting is prohibited at such sites. There are some exceptions along beaches where the emphasis is on maintaining the environment.

3   Any finds of precious metals, rings or other jewellery which are likely to be the result of personal loss, require the finder to take the item into the police station where details would be taken and if the item is not claimed, it will become either Crown property or be returned to the finder.

4   Jersey has a Custom & Excise Law which protects objects of historic interest. These can only be removed from the island with a licence. Generally, any item that appears to be aged fifty years or more, you will need a Custom Licence which allows the item to be exported after it has been assessed by the Jersey Heritage Trust at La Houge Bie Museum to determine its relevance to the island's history and the museum may choose to buy the find to prevent its removal.

Eire

In the Republic of Ireland The National Monuments (Amendment) Act 1987 (Section 2) states:

Subject to the provisions of this section a person shall not:

1a   Use or be in possession of a detection device in, or at the site of, a monument of which the Commissioners or a local authority are the owners or guardians or in respect of which a preservation order is in force or which stands registered in the Register or

2a   in an archaeological area that stands registered in the Register or

3a   in a Registered area

        OR

b   Use, at a place other than a place specified in paragraph a of this subsection, a detection device for the purpose of searching for archaeological objects or

c   Promote, whether by advertising or otherwise, the sale or use of detection devices for the purpose of searching for archaeological objects

Note: 'Archaeological area' is defined as 'an area which the Commissioners consider to be of archaeological importance but does not include the area of a historical monument standing entered in the Register'

Section 40 states that 'Where in a prosecution for an offence under this section it is proved that a detection device was used, it shall be presumed until the contrary is proved that the device was being used for the purpose of searching for archaeological objects'.

France

The experiences of battlefield walkers in France varies considerably. Regular visitors sometimes complain of harassment by local police forces but this does seem to be confined to people suspected of being relic hunters, especially in northern France around the old Western Front. It is perhaps understandable in an area where tourism is founded on the historical significance of the sites that the locals want to protect them.

Tales of arrest and confiscation of equipment by authorities contrast sharply with others of kindness and assistance provided by the ordinary people of the region. To get some idea of the nature of the problem, a visit to the forums can be useful (www.1914-1918. invisionzone.com).

Fieldwalking is less restricted than metal detecting, mainly because it doesn't involve equipment and is therefore harder to spot. However, the following rules apply across the board and it is safest to accept that the collection of any artefact without permission is technically illegal.

The use of metal detectors in France was, for many years, controlled by the use of the war time Patrimony Act 1941. However, on the 18 December 1989, Law Number 89-900 (NOR: MCCX8900 163L) was enacted. This lays down specific guidance around the use of metal detecting equipment and includes conditions that:

Article 1: No one may use metal detecting equipment for the purpose of searching for any monuments or objects relating to prehistory, history, art or archaeology without administrative authorization. This can be issued after consideration of an application based on the qualifications, purpose and nature of the survey to be undertaken and a licence can be issued by the Prefect of the region. Any application must be accompanied by the written consent of the owner of the land to be searched

Article 2: All publicity and instructions on the use of metal detectors must include the warning stated in Article 1, the penalties involved and the reason for this legislation. Failure to do so carries the penalty of a fine

Article 3: Every infringement of the present law will be noted by dealt with by law enforcement agencies under Article 3 of law number 80-532 (dated 15 July 1980) relating to the protection of public collections against acts of vandalism

Article 4: Reports of any infringments will be submitted by the law enforcement agencies laid out in Article 3 to the public prosecutor of the Republic in the jurisdiction where the offence was committed. Conviction will lead to a fine and confiscation of the equipment

Areas of particular importance, such as Verdun, are especially strict in enforcing these rules. It has yet to be tested but, to date, beaches are believed to be outside this law.

Belgium and the Netherlands

The general feeling seems to be that the Belgians are much more relaxed about their battlefield sites than the French, within reason of course. With that said, the current legal status of fieldwork is unclear. Across Europe, anti-terrorism legislation is being rushed into place which will inevitably impact on battlefield archaeology – an explosive device is still an explosive device, even when it is old. Advice should be sought from the local authorities before setting out.

OBTAINING PERMISSION

Whatever sort of survey you plan to undertake, the key is the co-operation of the landowner. All land is owned in England and Wales, either privately or in the hands of the state at some level or other. Often it is a fairly simple matter to ask permission of the landowner but finding whose field you are interested in may sometimes be a slightly trickier matter. Some land is rented or owned by someone living some distance away and ownership may not be obvious. If in doubt, try approaching people whose land borders the site and you may be redirected by them. Alternatively, an application to the land registry office covering that area will, for a fee, provide the information – for details, contact your local office or go to the registry's website (www.landregistry.gov.uk).

As ever, the use of a properly set out research design will be useful in securing permission – as we have seen, in France it will be vital. It could also be useful in securing the support of a local or regimental museum, which in turn can add weight to your request for permission to search.

PLANNING THE SEARCH

We have already discussed the development of a research design. Now is the time to review it. In approaching people for permission to enter their land, you need to be able to explain to them what will happen. Again, the six questions that form the basis of the research design need to be considered:

1 Who?   Who are you and who will be working with you? Do you have any special skills/qualifications/experience that will help convince the landowner that you should be let loose on their property? Who will be on hand to give expert advice when it is needed? Who is supporting the work?

2 What?   What is it that you plan to do? Fieldwalking is non-invasive and will only affect surface finds. Metal detecting will involve digging into the topsoil. Will this cause damage to the land? If so, how much and who will be responsible for making good? What are you looking for and what will happen if you find it? What is the legal situation regarding finds? If something valuable turns up, who gets it?

3 Where?   Where is it that you want to go and how will you get there? Do you need parking spaces that may block access to other areas?

4 Why?   Why is it important that you search? Why should the landowner give permission – what does he/she stand to gain from it?

5 When?   When do you plan to start? Fieldwalking is best done on ploughed land but could be harmful to new crops. The land is probably being used by the owner and you need to negotiate access around their schedule, not yours.

6 How?   How will the team be managed and the search carried out? How will finds be processed?

Having answers to all these will help to convince people that you are acting in good faith and that there is a real purpose to what you are doing. It also helps to make you and your team more confident that you will be able to produce a piece of research that will improve knowledge about your site and the period to which it belongs. Now you are ready to go on site.

6

SURVEYING THE BATTLEFIELD

Fans of television archaeology will be familiar with some of the high-tech equipment currently available, from ever-present geophysical surveys to computer-modeled reconstructions. If you have access to these, you probably don't need this book. However, the fact is that such equipment is scarce and expensive. Most fieldwork is undertaken by enthusiastic amateurs with minimal technology but able to bring something just as valuable, as Anthony Brown has pointed out:

> … detailed local knowledge, and a substantial input of time. Indeed, there can quite quickly come a point in anyone's fieldwork where the technology ceases to be useful and the traditional attributes of powers of observation, persistence, shrewdness, patience and enthusiasm are the ones required; we are dealing with art, not science (1987: 9).

As an example, he points to the work of Hollowell (1971), in which a Northamptonshire market gardener, working alone in the Nene Valley area, located some forty-four Iron Age and eighty-eight Roman sites over a fifteen-year period without specialised equipment.

We have already seen that most battlefield evidence is to be expected in the topsoil level and so this chapter is about conducting a survey of that layer by two very simple means: fieldwalking and metal detecting. The two can be used separately or together as part of a thorough sample of the surface of the site. We will look at how this can be achieved later. For now, though, they need to be defined.

FIELDWALKING

Fieldwalking, also sometimes referred to as 'surface collection', is the simplest form of archaeology and consists of exactly that – walking across a field to see what turns up. The aim is to try to identify what artefacts may lie further down in the soil and to locate their distribution across the site. Provided it is carried out systematically, fieldwalking can provide valuable information about deployments on the battlefield and allows for work to extend beyond the presently defined boundaries of known battlefield sites.

54 Marking out the grid during a field walking exercise

Like metal detecting, fieldwalking involves the removal of artefacts from the ground but it is much less controversial (archaeology being what archaeologists say it is). The main reason given is that fieldwalking only affects those artefacts already disturbed by ploughing and which are exposed to erosion and decay anyway. The 'iron harvest' of northern France is a prime example of how battlefield debris will continue to surface even after years of regular ploughing. In fact, as Drewett (1980) showed, a mid-1970s study of Sussex identified that 250 of 660 known archaeological sites in the area were being destroyed by deep ploughing before any recording work of any kind could be carried out (see also Hinchcliffe and Schadla-Hall, 1980). As a result of ploughing, artefacts are regularly brought to the surface and risk being lost if not collected when the opportunity arises.

The best time to conduct fieldwalking is some weeks after ploughing has taken place, once the soil has been broken up by frost and weathering. Newly ploughed soil is difficult to traverse and unlikely to reveal much, but after it has been left to settle, the soil will become more even and finds easier to spot. Intensive farming makes it harder to choose a time to carry out fieldwalking these days but generally between October and March are the best times to aim for, before new crops are ready for sowing. Ideally, an overcast day in late winter or early spring gives the best light because harsh sunlight creates deeper shadows in the furrows and so makes finds harder to spot, as does frost, snow and leaf fall near hedges. These factors need to be considered when recording the survey, as we will see below.

A complete survey can be extremely time-consuming. So in many cases, to save aching backs, sampling is used to provide an indication of what may be present without the need to cover 100 per cent of the target area. Between 10 and 20 per cent is usually enough for this purpose in most cases, but this will obviously depend on what you need your results for. An aircraft crash site or small-scale skirmish will be far more concentrated than a whole battlefield and it may be appropriate to consider a complete collection from these smaller sites.

METAL DETECTING

In marked contrast to fieldwalking, metal detecting is regarded by many as, at best, a necessary evil. From its origins among a few enthusiasts armed with Army surplus mine detectors, it has grown to a popular pastime for thousands of people, working alone or in groups. The publicity around a number of valuable finds has encouraged an image of the hobby as 'treasure hunting' and the result has been a competitive ethos among many detectorists to unearth as much as possible, as fast as possible. Large-scale rallies held at sites around the country encourage this and sales of battlefield relics on the Internet and at militaria sales bear witness to the amount of material that has been stripped from sites, usually without any reference to work that may be underway. Simon Richardson, who has worked for some time on the Towton battlefield in cooperation with the Towton Battlefield Archaeological Survey, has systematically recorded his finds but is frustrated by 'nighthawks' working the fields without permission. He cites cases in which heraldic devices that would have helped locate particular individuals during the battle have turned up in nearby antique shops – any information they could offer, lost (personal communication 2004).

Used properly, however, metal detectors can be an extremely useful tool in finding objects below the surface of unploughed fields. In order to try to develop better working practices, the National Council for Metal Detecting (NCMD) has issued guidelines for its members (Appendix C) and is working closely with established battlefield archaeologists to develop the use of detectorists as team members.

PREPARING THE SURVEY

Before survey work can begin, a couple of issues need to be addressed. The first is that of obtaining the landowner's permission. All land is owned, even common land, which may be subject to by-laws. Secondly, an agreement needs to be made regarding any finds. In the case of valuable items, the agreement is usually an equal sharing of any profit. In addition, although the land may be owned and permission given, there is still the question of how the site is regarded by the authorities. Ancient monuments and other recorded sites are an obvious example but there have been prosecutions by the Ministry of Defence against amateur archaeologists recovering the wreck of an aircraft which contained human remains, even with the consent of the next of kin and the landowner, as the site was regarded as a war grave. Check what permissions and agreements are needed and get them in writing if at all possible.

PREPARING THE TEAM

Assuming you're lucky enough to have some willing volunteers handy, you now need to brief them about what is going to happen. You need to ensure that every member of the team understands:

1   The use of a grid in the survey and how this will be recorded
2   The importance of charting the location of artefacts during the survey
3   What they are looking for and any safety implications
4   The labelling system to be used
5   How to record their work

This may appear obvious, but a significant failing of many archaeologists, especially in sites where experienced members allow themselves to become focused on one aspect or other, is to ignore the help. The more someone feels part of the team, the better the results will be. That means that to get the best out of your helpers, you need to be willing and able to answer questions about finds, to explain what you are doing and why it is important and help others to share your enthusiasm.

PREPARING THE SITE

Whichever survey method is to be used, site preparation will be the same. A grid needs to be established across the site so that finds can be accurately and systematically located and recorded. This can be done with minimal equipment consisting of:

1. A set of bamboo canes, sufficient to mark out a grid pattern across the site. The actual number will depend on the size of the site and of the grid you want to establish. These canes should be marked with three different colours of tape or paint – two to identify the grid, the third to identify specific finds within the grid.
2. A rope or measure marked out at 10 or 20m intervals.
3. A large-scale map of the site (available from Ordnance Survey outlets).
4. A selection of sealable plastic bags (the kind used for sandwiches are fine but stronger versions can be bought from metal detector suppliers).
5. Waterproof, airtight containers ('Tupperware') to protect delicate finds (or bubblewrap).
6. Waterproof marker pens to record finds and bag numbers. (A tag with the grid square number placed inside the bag acts as insurance in case the outside notes get destroyed).
7. A sense of humour.

If possible, the use of a satellite positioning system will greatly speed up the process and enable you to pinpoint locations accurately, but it isn't strictly necessary.

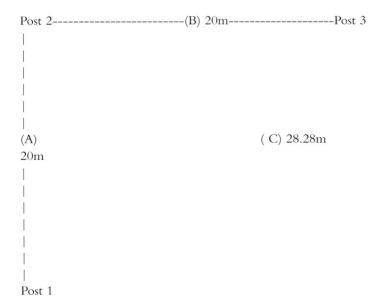

Diagram 1: Using the Pythagoran formula, $A^2+B^2 =C^2$, Post 1 will be on a diagonal line 28.28m from Post 3

Step 1

The first step is to establish a baseline along the longest side of the site for the grid. The obvious starting point would be a track edge or similar obvious feature. However, bear in mind that land changes over time and you need to ensure that you can return to the same spot, possibly years from now. The first marker needs to be very carefully placed and marked on the large-scale map. Everything else will be measured from here.

Step 2

The size of the grid will vary according to the site and the type of search. In a large area, 20m squares allow fieldwalking and metal detecting to be carried out at the same time, but for something like a crash site, smaller squares may give better information. In either case, a row of canes should be placed at the appropriate interval along the baseline, alternating the colour of the cane to make it easier to follow each line across the field.

There are many ways of setting out the grid from here. Some use Pythagoras' formula ($a^2+b^2=c^2$) to lay out a series of triangles. If the first cane acts as the base, then a second cane is placed 20m along the baseline. Using this formula, a right angled triangle would place the third cane at 20m from cane 2 and 28.28m from cane 1. By using a measure to mark out one line 20m from cane 2 and one 28.28m from cane 1, where the lines cross, is the position of cane 3. It is less complicated than it sounds (see below). This may seem like an odd way when you could simply measure outwards from each cane, but that risks the line drifting apart and this method keeps it consistent and straight.

Alternatively, if there are enough people available, a rope marked at 20m intervals can be laid on the ground along the baseline. An alternately coloured cane is then inserted behind the rope, so that it doesn't get tangled as you move forward. At each end, it is moved forward 20m and the process repeated across the field. Of course, few fields are conveniently regular shapes, but the main grid can be marked out and the remaining area marked as a continuation of the grid. Each corner of the whole grid needs to be marked accurately on the large-scale map and it should then be possible to add an acetate or tracing paper grid over the map to match what is laid out in the field before you.

Step 3

By now, you should have rows of differently coloured canes stretching across the field from your baseline. These rows are known as 'transects'. Each transect is marked at 20m intervals and these form squares referred to as 'stints'.

The next task is to assign a numbering system to the grid. Some people opt for the obvious 'Transect 1/Stint A/Stint B', etc.. This allows finds to be quickly located e.g. 'cartridge case 1/A'. However, this method has its limitations. Swift (2003) describes using a system based on an arbitrary number, such as 500 for the transect and 500/501/502 for the stints. This has the advantage of being flexible enough to account for finds outside the target area without complicating the matter by using negative numbers. As long as the system is clearly explained in your recording, the actual system is not that important.

Step 4

The grid is now in place. Team members need to be clearly briefed about what they are looking for and issued finds bags. Separate bags need to be issued for surface finds and metal detector finds, and clearly marked as to which is which. In particular, members need to know what to do with finds. As Fox and Scott (1991) have shown from their work at Little Big Horn, a great deal can be achieved by examining the distribution of bullets and casings. It is important not to pick up such items until their exact position has been noted, so this is where the third colour of cane is used. Particular pieces of evidence, or items that the finder is uncertain of, should be marked by a cane so that they can be recorded before they are recovered. The finds bags can be used for other, more general finds and the finds from each stint should be placed in a separate plastic bag.

Step 5

As each stint is completed, flagged finds should be recorded by the person best able to identify finds. If a GPS or similar satellite system is available, this can be a fairly

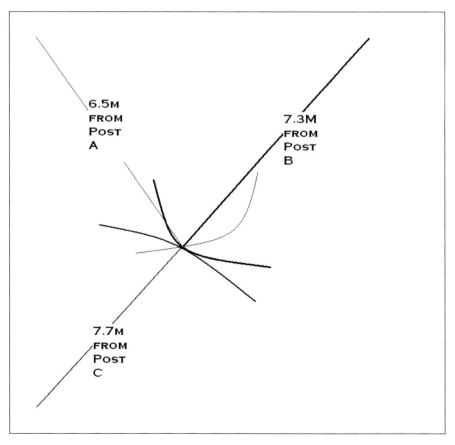

Diagram 2 Plotting the location using a compass. By measuring from the marker posts, the distance can be set using a compass and pencil. Where the arcs cross is the location of the find

straightforward job. If not, measurements should be taken from the nearest canes. Using a compass, a circle can be drawn on the map at that distance. A second circle from the next cane, will cross the first, indicating the location on the map grid so it can be recorded accurately. The type of find can then be added to the map as a symbol marked with the find number. This needs to be done for each find so that later, the pattern of distribution of various finds can be plotted.

Plotting finds:

	Stint A	Stint B	Stint C	Stint D
Transect 4	□ □			
Transect 3		• •	# #	• • •
Transect 2	•	•		° °° ° ° ° +++ +++
Transect 1				

• = Rifle casing   □ = Pistol casing   # = Grenade fragments   + = Machine gun casings
° = Mortar fragments

Recording finds like this on tracing paper or acetate allows a map of their locations to be overlaid onto an ordinary map to tie together the geography with the archaeology. Here, for example, we can piece together the possible story of an assault on a machinegun position by a rifle section. We can theorise that the gun group was perhaps hit by mortar fragments early in the attack and were finished off by rifle fire in a very rapid action.

DEALING WITH FINDS

There are a number of books available on the subject of finds and conservation but their quality varies. A reliable and accessible guide has been produced for metal detectorists by Richard Hobbs, Celia Honeycombe and Sarah Watkins (*Guide to Conservation for Metal Detectorists* Tempus 2002) and is a good starting point to ensure that finds are recovered and protected effectively. Alongside their advice the Portable Antiquities Scheme, set up with funding from the National Lottery, provides contact details for archaeologists whose job it is to liaise with the public and assist in identifying finds. They are able to offer advice and information about the recovery of finds and how best to conserve them once lifted out of the ground. It is important to take advice rather than to rely on written information since methods and best practice change rapidly. The first rule must be — if in any doubt about the best way to lift a find, or if the find is fragile, part of a hoard or some larger object, then always seek advice.

In the field, it can be very tempting to try to do too much, too quickly. Place each find in a marked bag, giving date and as exact a location as possible. If the object is wet, keep it wet and away from any dry finds. Collect everything that is not obviously rubbish — junk can always be discarded later after it has been checked — and store in the plastic containers. Foam padding or bubblewarp can protect fragile items, but do not allow them to be in direct contact as this may affect the object. Backfill any holes immediately and do not dig below the level of ploughing in disturbed soil.

Detectorists often develop a number of potentially harmful habits, such as rubbing an object on their sleeve to clean it. It may be that the soil around it is all that is holding it together! The surrounding soil may actually contain further clues, so a find should not be cleaned in the field if possible. It certainly shouldn't be washed in the nearest puddle or stream and definitely not put in your pocket with all the other bits and pieces you find that day.

Once home and in a safe environment, each object can be dealt with. In general, most finds can be air dried by leaving them in egg boxes or something similar which will allow them to dry evenly. Do not attempt to dry them using heat of any kind as this could cause them to crack. Once dried, they can be sealed in plastic bags with silica gel to contain any condensation that might form until they can be sent to their destination or mounted for display. Do not be tempted to use cleaning agents, as these can speed corrosion even more.

Always wash your hands before and after handling finds, firstly to ensure that you do not contaminate the artefact and, secondly to make sure it doesn't contaminate you. Certain types of corrosive residue are toxic. Never, for example, brush lead musket balls without a face mask and always be aware of Health and Safety issues for whatever substance you are working with. Assess what the object is and what it may be made of before deciding whether to dry it, or wash it gently in a tub of water to remove excess dirt, but never under the tap. If there are any other fragile finds attached, the tub means you will find them — you won't if they disappear down the drain.

What is vital is the ability to recognise finds for what they are. In the case of modern equipment, there are a number of excellent and detailed guides available and it is worth

55 An expert handles explosives uncovered during work on the Somme

investing in some of these beforehand. British webbing of the First and Second World Wars contained a bewildering array of buckles and the ability to identify the difference between those likely to be lost easily and those that form a more integral part of the set may be significant in the field.

Metallic finds

Soldiers call it 'pink mist'. This is what happens to the human body when it comes into contact with high explosives at the wrong time. As one ex-trooper put it, 'you're not only history, you're geography as well'. It is a weird trait of the civilian world to assume that weapons only affect those they are meant to. Every year, farmers and souvenir hunters are harmed by ammunition that has been lying around for nearly a century. So the constant rule has to be that you should treat any weapons find as dangerous. Police and customs in Britain are now taking the issue of battlefield relics extremely seriously and great care needs to be taken if you are working on a site with the potential to contain explosives or chemical weapons – since sniffer dogs probably do not distinguish between modern and historical explosives and you could end up with some serious explaining to do.

Any obviously spent cases, being made of brass, will survive, but weapons, shell, grenade or mortar fragments are likely to contain iron, which rusts quickly and it is often difficult to recognise heavily rusted pieces. So real care needs to be taken in ensuring that as much evidence as possible is retained. Do not wash it but allow it to air dry. Smaller pieces can be placed in plastic bags or Tupperware containers with silica

56 Items need careful identification. Different types of the same weapon may indicate a different time in the war

57 Forensic archaeologists examine bone fragments

58 Horse skull, Thiepval Wood. Possibly the remains of a pack animal killed by shellfire. Not an obvious casualty but one that needs to be considered for what it can tell us about transport in the area

59 Finds processing

gel once dried. Once the item is stabilised, then you can explore options for further cleaning and identification.

Leather and textiles

The chances of finding organic materials after any length of time are slim but in boggy terrain, it is a possibility. Special care needs to be taken to ensure that if they are wet when found, then they can be placed in plastic bags, kept wet and out of sunlight for transport back to specialist conservation advice. If dry, then they should be kept dry and should not be placed directly into plastic because of the condensation risk. Do not handle them more than necessary, as the skin secretes acidic oils which may harm the find. Store in Tupperware in a cool, dark place – the fridge is ideal, but the freezer will be too cold.

Human remains

The recovery of human remains is the most controversial aspect of battlefield archaeology. Many argue, perhaps rightly, that the fallen should be left in peace and consider any undertaking that might impact on this as disrespectful. The ethical issues are for you to decide. Nevertheless, it is a sad fact that many thousands of bodies still lie in unmarked graves around the world and even here in the UK. Few researchers are ghoulish enough to set out looking for bodies for the fun of it, but any research into a battlefield carries with it the possibility that human remains may be uncovered.

Andy Robertshaw, Curator of the Royal Logistics Corps Museum, whose work with a team of archaeologists on the Western Front over many years has involved recovering remains, argues that it is important that where bodies are found, they are recovered properly. He said:

> This was a time before the Army issued dog-tags … and a lot of guys went into battle with their names written on scraps of paper in their pockets because they didn't want to be forgotten or lost. If we don't try our best to recover these men and to do what we can to identify them, it's like we're killing them twice (personal communication, 2005).

Fraser (2006), another member of the team, has demonstrated just how much information can be recovered and how this can be used to finally bring closure to a family. It's a difficult argument to ignore and one that cannot be dismissed out of hand, as many of the critics of battlefield archaeology seem to want to do.

Recovering a human body in such a way as to offer some chance of identifying it is a delicate task and should not be attempted without experience and advice. In the first instance, there is always the question of whether it is a casualty in the first place. Where better to hide a murder victim than on a battlefield filled with other skeletons? For the amateur archaeologist, the first response has to be to call the police. The removal of a body from the ground requires a special licence and skilled handling. Mark the site carefully and avoid moving about more than necessary. Later, if you are able to negotiate with the authorities, it may be that you can take part in the recovery process yourself but, as far as possible, you should always avoid disturbing the dead merely out of curiosity.

RECORDING THE WORK

We have already discussed the need to record the site, the grid and the finds in a systematic way. The finds have all been logged according to which transect and which stint they belong, and finds of particular interest have been plotted on an overlay of the large-scale map. Alongside this, a note should be made of:

1 The number of people taking part.
2 The weather conditions on the day.
3 The time spent on the search.
4 The soil conditions.
5 Any problems encountered.

This will be useful information later. If, in a few years' time, researchers look at your findings and conclude that a certain field is not going to offer any information based on the fact that you only recovered a few items, they may not be aware that there were only two people involved and half an hour into the search you were forced off the site by a blizzard. A record of the conditions and the time spent provides a much fuller impression of not only what work has been done, but how well it was done.

7

EXPERIMENTAL ARCHAEOLOGY: LIVING THE PAST

In the Introduction to this book, we noted that Clive Gamble defines archaeology as 'basically about three things: objects, landscapes and what we make of them. It is quite simply the study of the past through material remains'. Finding artefacts, as we have seen, can be as simple as walking across a field and picking them up. Understanding what we have picked up and why they are significant is where the real skill lies.

In 1954, American Anthropologist Christopher Hawkes examined the kind of information we are able to infer about the past and identified four levels:

TECHNOLOGY

The type of artefacts discovered at a site provides information about the technology available at the time. This is a fairly straightforward aspect of archaeology – if only flint tools are found, we can be as certain as we can be that this site was used during a particular period in which more sophisticated tools were not available.

Artefacts from the battlefield will tell us what weapons were in use and give an indication of the possible numbers. By recovering and identifying musket balls, the various types of weapon can be plotted across the site. The presence of carbine and pistol balls can indicate a cavalry action, for example. The absence of a particular calibre may be equally significant in highlighting supply problems to an army.

SUBSISTENCE

At the very roots of survival are the basic needs of food, water and shelter. Again, the artefacts will tell us a great deal about the way people interacted and met these needs at the time. They will also tell us about the networks of trade that existed among groups. The presence of objects that can only have come from a considerable distance have frequently been found on sites where we might expect travel to be limited at best, but Roman and Viking sites regularly produce items that must have been transported over

60 The arrival of the musket significantly changed the face of warfare as fighting forces began to disperse to present fewer targets

thousands of miles to reach their final destination. Again, this type of information can be used with certainty to identify the types of economic behaviour, diet and trade carried out in any particular period.

In wartime, survival takes on a new significance. The basic needs of food and shelter become complicated by the added factor of obtaining these without being killed in the process. Consequently, battlefield archaeology shifts into a study of how the sometimes conflicting demands of security and comfort can be met by armies at all levels. For the simple soldier, it is a matter of personal survival – for his commander, it is a problem of ensuring that as many men as possible reach the point at which the enemy can kill them instead of the weather or disease.

POLITICAL AND SOCIAL ORGANISATION

The third of Hawkes' inferences is a much harder subject to tackle. Human social organization takes many forms and inferences based on modern pre-industrial societies can only supply possible examples. Where written records exist this becomes easier, but the fact remains that even these sources concern primarily the literate, powerful classes at the expense of the ordinary citizen.

Civil war is commonplace. In investigating such fighting, we need to look at the patterns of allegiance and neutrality within an area to understand how the social and political organization of a society reacts to war. In an earlier chapter, it was pointed out that in the English Civil War period, neutrals formed a large bloc and, although common people could find themselves conscripted, fighting was largely confined to those with particular personal reason for doing so. Within communities, conscription was used to rid the area of the unemployed or criminals before ordinary citizens were compelled to serve. Identifying who fights and why is a crucial element to understanding their actions.

Written accounts of war offer a fairly comprehensive picture of how armies were organised throughout recorded history but still gaps remain in our understanding. Equally, myths about the social organisation of armies have emerged that give a misleading impression of how events actually unfurled. At a First World War cemetery in France, one of the authors overheard a group of British schoolchildren being asked by their teacher to inspect the graves and to note that there were so few officers' graves and no senior officers at all. The inference, based on years of a 'lions led by donkeys' mythology, was that the ordinary soldier was sent to his death by remote generals. Imagine, though, that by some terrible mishap the school party met with a disaster that caused fatalities. By the same token, could we ask why there might be relatively few teachers among the casualties and no members of the local authority's education department, or would we simply acknowledge that there would be a staff/pupil ratio that meant there would inevitably be fewer teachers than pupils among the victims? In fact, research shows that the casualty rate among all officers, even very senior ones, was proportionately higher than for other ranks with around 200 British generals (an

61 Re-enactment helps
to gain an understanding
of how it felt to live as a
soldier

average of one per week) dying in action during the war, often further forward than
their duties required them to be. Corrigan (2003) has provided a useful counterbalance
to this mythology that helps to dispel some of the assumptions made about the social
organisation of the British Army of the early twentieth century, but these and other
myths continue to risk acting as a restrictive influence on the interpretation of the
evidence available. Much work remains to be undertaken about the role of hierarchies
within armies. For example, at Agincourt, social standing was a crucial factor in the
behaviour of the French Army but we know relatively little about how the English
formed and deployed, relying instead on what Alfred Burne has called 'inherent military
probability' (1996: xix) to fill in the gaps.

We need also to recognise how the closed environment of the regiment can develop
very definite ideologies which can be difficult for civilians to understand (see, for an
extreme example, Jennings & Weale 1996). Marshall's 1947 study of the behaviour of
US troops in battle during the Second World War led the way in the study of the
psychological and social factors affecting the way in which soldiers cope with their
environment. More recently, Hockey's (1986) study of the sociology of military training
shows how social organisation within a unit forms, along with the impact this may have
on behaviour in battle. During the filming of the BBC series *The Trench*, directing staff

62 Recent years have seen a sharp increase in understanding of the psychological and social impact of war

noted with interest that the volunteers very quickly became involved in the project to the point where some submitted to recreated punishments, even though they were entirely free to refuse, because to do so would be to let down the other volunteers (Van Emden 2002).

Anderton (2002) has applied the significance of social organisation to his study of twentieth-century coastal defences by noting how the layout of the camp reflects the hierarchy of control within the military. The relative status of buildings within the confines of the camp stands as a powerful symbol of control over the men, controlling the surrounding countryside in much the same way as did the medieval keep.

RELIGIOUS ORGANISATION

The presence of druids at Stonehenge to mark the solstice belies the fact that it is a religion based entirely on modern assumptions of what druidism was actually about. No written record exists to support how rituals should be performed. The only sources available are those produced by the Romans, who destroyed druidism in the first place and are therefore not the most objective source. The study of existing religious belief systems is a cornerstone of Social Anthropology and texts frequently refer to apparently bizarre beliefs that can only be understood within the context of the society itself. The so-called 'Cargo Cults' of the South Pacific are a prime example of this. In a society founded on the importance of trade and 'cargo', the sudden arrival during the Pacific Campaign of the Second World War of huge amounts of military equipment, and particularly the presence of black troops seemingly rich beyond the wildest dreams of the islanders, created the conditions for a new pattern of belief to arise. In the years following the war, islanders began to construct airfields and even enacted rituals in which pieces of paper were handed to a man acting as airfield controller, who would then speak into a cast-off radio and wait for the planes to arrive. Cultists still perform military-style parades and look to a god they call 'Jon Frum' (said to derive from a greeting by US troops, 'Hi, I'm John From America'). Even with the arrival of new technology to the islands, the belief has simply adapted and the John Frum cult now has a hopeful website requesting 'cargo', or cash equivalent (www.enzo.nz/jonfrum). In an article for the *Smithsonian Magazine*, Paul Raffaele (Feb 2006), described a meeting with the cult's leader, Chief Isaac:

> John promised you much cargo more than 60 years ago, and none has come', I point out. 'So why do you keep faith with him? Why do you still believe in him?' Chief Isaac shoots me an amused look. 'You Christians have been waiting 2,000 years for Jesus to return to earth,' he says, 'and you haven't given up hope.

Where religious faith is involved we need to be aware that other, apparently illogical belief systems, are every bit as valid as our own and that we need to understand them within their own context. Without a guide to explain things, we are merely going to invent our own explanations for behaviours based on what we think we know about what we have today – clearly something that will not stand up to close scientific scrutiny.

In battlefield archaeology, we need to make some adaptations to Hawkes' work but the concept of levels of inference remains valid.

Some campaigns, such as the Crusades and the current fighting in the Middle East and elsewhere, have their roots in religious intolerance. It has been said that there are no atheists in the foxholes and religion will inevitably play some role in supporting or condemning any course of action. An understanding of its importance and its manipulation will greatly assist in an understanding of attitudes toward the function of war – the destruction of the enemy. This is most apparent through analysis of the rituals surrounding death and attitudes towards it among the troops involved in any action. Would the dead be treated with reverence or as a burden? Would, for example, the casualties of a civil war action be offered a 'decent Christian burial' or simply be buried anonymously in mass pits? Would men expect different treatment after death as 'heroes' or as common soldiers, compared to what they might expect as civilians? Evidence suggests that even where a churchyard stands nearby, most would simply be disposed of in a pit. Where, then, and why, do monuments to war dead begin to emerge? Harvey Schwartz (1984) has written of the profound impact contact with the dead has had on combat veterans of the Vietnam war and the significance of ritual in 'cleansing' warriors returning from war has been a noted feature of many pre-industrial societies (Holm 1990). Contemporary religious and social attitudes toward killing are again an important factor in assessing performance and actions in combat.

Where Hawkes refers to inferences about religion, it might be more appropriate within battlefield interpretation to turn to what, in the twenty-first century, appears to be becoming the new religion – psychology.

The late twentieth century has seen a major shift in our understanding of the mental impact of combat on those who experience it. In the UK we have lagged behind other countries in accepting the existence of combat-related trauma and even now, twenty-five years after it was first defined by the American Psychiatric Association, the issue of Post Traumatic Stress Disorder (PTSD) remains cloudy in Britain. The Ministry of Defence (MOD), by accident or design, has failed to recognise the operative word 'Post' – as in 'after'. PTSD, by its very definition, is a problem that develops some time after the event. In many cases this can mean years later. Veterans often throw themselves into rebuilding their interrupted civilian careers and it is only much later, in retirement, that they have time to reflect on their experiences.

By choosing to confuse the matter by referring to 'shell-shock', the MOD has been able to point to the relatively low numbers of soldiers affected in combat by psychological problems. 'Shell shock', or 'Acute Combat Reaction' as it is also known, is something that affects the soldier's ability to function in the war zone itself and can be effectively dealt with quickly, and as close to the front lines as possible. It is a significant difference. Behaviour in battle is directly affected by the individual's mental state at the time. We need to have this in mind when we try to interpret the artefacts uncovered. Are we dealing with an aggressive unit or one where the troops are nearing exhaustion? Is the lack of evidence in an obvious position the result of a failure to recognise its significance or due to the failure noted by Marshall (1947) of individuals to use their weapons actively when isolated on the battlefields? Equally, peer pressure plays a vital role in maintaining unit cohesion, as seen most poignantly in the example of the famous 'Pals' battalions on the Somme. We need to understand what factors eventually erode discipline to the point that mutinies or 'soldiers' strikes' might take place (Patsy Adam-Smith 1978: 319-21, for example, cites the ANZAC mutinies in 1918 and points to the breaking up of tightly knit units as being the trigger). To what degree were earlier soldiers able to take collective action and, given the allegedly harsh treatment of British soldiers fighting the revolutionary French Army of Napoleon, why did they choose to fight them rather than their own (British) oppressors?

There has been a tendency throughout archaeology to assume that our ancestors saw the world very differently to ourselves. There is also an assumption that the psychological impact of combat is a phenomenon of the late twentieth century. To an extent this is true. We are now more remote from combat than ever before and death has become something that few of us ever actually see. Yet the anecdotal evidence of exactly the same traumas and consequences crop up time and again in the written record. What we now know as survivor guilt is described in Homer's accounts of the Trojan War and

63 US Marine enactors

Pepys' diaries describe PTSD symptoms after the plague and fire of London. Whilst we need to put it in the context of what we know of social norms and values of the time, we need to credit historical figures with humanity and recognise that the retrospective application of our understanding of the human psyche, fraught though it is with risk, is a vital component of our interpretation of the behaviour of men in battle.

To some degree, experimental archaeology is able to offer some answers to the more concrete questions, but we have to accept that there are some areas that will forever be subject to interpretation and reinterpretation. There is a joke that asks how many Vietnam veterans it takes to change a light bulb: 'That's right, man, you don't know cos you weren't there ok!' As archaeologists and historians, we can never truly understand the experience of combat. So we can analyse the decisions made by commanders on the spot in the luxury of a safe, warm armchair with all the benefits of hindsight. In some cases, too much information is available about the outcome for us to really understand how an action unfolded. Experimental archaeology is a means by which we can at least try to gain experience that will help us to interpret the evidence more clearly.

In 1947, the Norwegian anthropologist Thor Heyerdahl built a balsa raft, 'Kon-Tiki', from a traditional design to see whether such a craft could sail from South America to Polynesia in the Pacific, in order to test a theory that traders from Latin America could have settled there. It was assumed by most researchers that such a voyage was impossible at the time because the boats were not considered capable of making the journey. Three months after setting out, Heyerdahl and his crew reached their goal. Later, using a papyrus-reed boat, the 'Ra', he demonstrated that Central and South America could have been reached by Mediterranean civilisations with equally primitive designs. Experiments like these have now become an accepted part of archaeological research but these experiments are not without their drawbacks. Not least, of course, is the fact that in recreating such journeys, we know that the destination actually exists and how long it should take to get there – a luxury not afforded to the original travellers. Just because they could make the journey, we cannot assume that they did.

ARTEFACTS

A number of experiments have been undertaken in recreating artefacts using traditional methods. Jonathon Coles (1979) has provided a useful introduction into the uses and drawbacks of experimental archaeology, but briefly we can consider that the chief drawback to any attempt to recreate even fairly recent technology is that we don't always know how it was done because it was so fundamental to everyday life that no one felt the need to describe it. Imagine, for example, how many teenagers today would be able to light a coal fire. Much of what we term 'common sense' is anything but that. Tasks we perform every day will, in another generation, be redundant and within two or three generations the skills to perform it will be forgotten.

In attempting to reproduce an object or an action, we lack the experience of the original user. A longbow would be used by someone whose body was deformed by constant practice over years with massive muscular development enabling him to draw back the heavy bow to achieve its maximum performance. We cannot recreate that. Equally, we are influenced by the modern concept of attempting to make our lives as 'efficient' as possible to maximise time. Our ancestors led a much slower lifestyle in which efficiency, in the time management sense, was not paramount. With that said, because the skills are lost, so, too, are the short cuts that our ancestors knew, as well as alternate uses for objects that we may not be able to recognise because we have never had to use them.

A hypothetical example of this can be taken from a very recent conflict. The Falklands war of 1982 took place in a remote location. There are many artefacts still lying on the old battlefields. Among these can be found brightly coloured 'bungees' — short elasticated ropes with metal hooks sold in caravan and camping supply shops. They are unmilitary-looking items but what could they be used for? The obvious answer is that they are found in camping supply shops, so they could relate to camping. That is a correct assumption. Rather than carrying heavy tents, troops use a waterproof poncho to create a 'basha' or improvised tent. The bungee acts as a guy rope and keeps the poncho taut so that it keeps the rain off. We can experiment with that and demonstrate its use. At the same time, bungees can also be used for holding equipment in place. The 1958 pattern webbing issued to troops at the time could tend to sag when loaded, making movement difficult. By threading a bungee through the top of each pouch and attaching each end to the webbing yoke, the whole lot could be held more tightly and comfortably to the body. Again, the value of this cannot be appreciated without experimentation. For the infantryman, every item is simply another piece of weight. Even a rifle sling is an additional burden, since, in combat, a slung rifle is of no use to its owner.

The role of experimental archaeology in dealing with artefacts is therefore to look at why an object might be carried, perhaps over long distances, before it can be used and the costs and benefits to the carrier of doing it.

SITES AND STRUCTURES

A number of experiments are currently ongoing to explore how structures were built and how they deteriorate when out of use, such as that at Ovenden Down where earthworks have been constructed and their steady decay monitored over decades. Other examples include the recreation of everything from Viking villages to First World War trench systems for use by re-enactment groups.

Heyerdahl's experiments have been followed by more recent examples using Viking longboats, Greek and Roman warships and various others. A major drawback to these experiments is the incomplete records of how they were used and the lack of anything by which to measure the accuracy of the reconstruction. They demonstrate that such structures could be used in a certain way, but they don't prove that they were used.

RE–ENACTMENT

Of all the activities that might fall under the umbrella of experimental archaeology, re-enactment is perhaps the most accessible and useful for the amateur archaeologist. From its beginnings as something of a fringe activity for eccentrics, the hobby of re-enactment or 'living history' has developed into a highly skilled and professional activity. Those who take part live for days at a time in their chosen period and are able to explain at first hand the everyday experiences of people throughout history.

Some groups have been able to obtain land away from public view on which they have recreated the relevant structures – be it an Iron Age farm, a Dark Ages village or a First World War trench – to enable them to live as closely as possible to the people of their period. This offers an ideal opportunity to try to develop the archaeological imagination but also to appreciate factors that may be decisive in battle.

Take, for example, footwear. It is only by attempting to climb a hill covered in wet grass, wearing chain mail, carrying a sword and with shoes that lack any sort of grip at all, that the difficulties faced by the Normans at Hastings can be fully appreciated. Equally, it is only by observing the 'fog of war' caused by powder smoke from a massed volley of musket fire that one begins to understand why, in one action during the American Civil War, a unit got into a rather one-sided firefight with a clump of bushes.

In 2001, the BBC used this form of experimentation to recreate the experiences of a unit of Pals from Hull in the First World War. With the assistance of a re-enactment group, they were able to replicate a section of trench and the training regime of the period. In his account of the exercise, Richard Van Emden (2002) reports how, even in an artificial environment in which the participants knew that they were in no real danger, superstitions began to develop around certain objects and rituals, just as they have been reported in contemporary accounts.

Living history groups offer an opportunity to explore artefacts in their everyday context and, at the same time, explore how people interact with objects. Whilst working on a project involving members of the American Civil War Society, one of the authors was able to note that most experienced members carried very little equipment, confining themselves to only what was absolutely necessary, whilst other, newer members were frequently draped like cartoon bandits in knives and weapons. It was, apparently, exactly what had happened in the real thing. Those who had discarded everything but the basics were those who had taken part in a long route march in high summer. A trail of items had been left behind for the support team to load into a vehicle following behind and a valuable lesson was learned.

WARGAMING

Yet another form of experimentation comes through using wargames to simulate and interpret actions and behaviour. These can range in scale from small unit actions to full scale campaigns and perhaps reached their peak in the wargame conducted at Sandhurst in the 1970s, in which the men charged with defending Britain in 1940 were pitted against their German counterparts. The invasion, it seems, would have failed.

Wargaming allows a number of 'what if' scenarios to be explored and can be a useful way to consider issues already raised here about why a particular location was chosen as against another. A field survey to determine angles of sight and terrain difficulties,

64 Experimental archaeology also incorporates the rebuilding of equipment like these jeeps

65 A peaceful country scene, but this was once the site of the bloodiest battle on English soil
– Bloody Meadow, Towton. Note the river in the valley and prehistoric farm terraces on the hillside

followed by a re-enactment of that particular action, can provide clear and vital information about decisions and their consequences.

We have seen, then, that experimental archaeology can take many forms. For the amateur, lacking the funds to rebuild and sail a full-size HMS *Victory* to test a theory, living history groups offer perhaps the best means by which to develop the archaeological imagination and to understand the experience of the soldiers on the field on the day. It is that appreciation that moves research from the abstract to the real. Without that understanding, there is no context by which to make judgments about the action you are studying and no measure by which to discuss victory or defeat, heroism or cowardice.

PRESENTING YOUR FINDINGS

There is a growing interest in understanding not only the immediate impact of war, but also the way in which wars are commemorated. Whilst battles may have a tremendous significance to history, those who died in them could, until very recently, expect no recognition of their contribution. Often, the dead would be piled into unmarked mass graves or even left to rot where they fell. It was not until mass conscription in the twentieth century finally forced millions of civilians into the military that their loss began to matter to the public at large. The First World War saw the widespread development of memorials, as well as in the following decades of mass battlefield tourism (Oliver 2005). Today, the fields of France and Flanders have been described as a 'memorial landscape'. The question for the battlefield archaeologist is one of providing clarity about what it is that is actually being commemorated by the project being undertaken.

Cultural memory, the cornerstone of the heritage industry, is where history is reduced to story. Because the heritage industry is just that, an industry, it must produce a profit. It does this by offering an acceptable, even desirable, version of the reality of the past with the boringly objective bits cut out. The legend of Robin Hood and the attendant 'heritage experiences' are big business and bring tourism to Nottinghamshire, without any reference to the simple fact that the original stories of Robin Hood make no reference to Nottingham. In fact, all the evidence shows that a 'Robert' or 'Robin' Hood lived in Wakefield and the dates of his life tie with the first written references to Robin operating at Barnsdale, near Pontefract – at that time, part of the forest of Sherwood and under the jurisdiction of the Sheriff of Nottingham. We can therefore choose to commemorate a real person living as an outlaw in Yorkshire or a pantyhose-wearing storybook fop in Lincoln Green. There's no competition.

We need to consider this when preparing to present the results of research. What is the market for the information you have gathered? Who do you want to present it to? It has been said that static museum displays are like art galleries – you need to know what you're looking at before you appreciate what it is. The alternative is to present a 'dumbed down' version to get people interested and then try to increase awareness of the detail. In considering what to do with the information you have pieced together, you need to consider what sort of compromises you are willing to make in order to put it in the public domain.

Schofield (2005) provides an excellent discussion of the issues that have arisen in the field of heritage management. This book, however, is about amateur archaeology more than the development of a professional approach to presenting history through heritage and museum projects. As such, it is assumed that the main route by which the results will be made public is through written reports.

Once all the evidence has been gathered, the last step in the process is to present the results. A great deal of valuable work has been undertaken in archaeology in general, and battlefield archaeology in particular, but much of what it has to tell us is wasted because no record has been made available. At the research design stage you should have made some decisions about what sort of record you intended to make of the study – whether you plan a book or an article for a military history publisher, a local history, an academic thesis or just feedback to those who have helped you finish your work.

Now, having gathered the evidence, it's time to look again at what record you want to produce. Peter White (2006) quotes the famous archaeologist Sir Mortimer Wheeler, who said that 'plain and effective writing requires a plain and effective structure' (1956: 215) and argues in favour of a simple narrative structure of:

1 Introduction and aims.
2 Background.
3 Methods.
4 Results.
5 Discussion and conclusions.

In universities, this is sometimes abbreviated to an even simpler 'tell'em what you're going to say. Say it. Then tell 'em what you've said'. This structure allows the reader to follow the logical processes behind the work and to be able to focus on any one aspect of the report. The structure is also flexible enough to adapt to almost any audience, whether it be an academic piece for archaeologists or a simple report to the local parish council. Following White, we can expand on this:

INTRODUCTION

Frequently the hardest part of any piece of writing, the introduction should be a broad outline of what the work you have done was for, and why. Many writers prefer to draft this out very roughly before coming back to it after the main body is complete because, in all probability, the finished piece will have significant differences to your original ideas.

BACKGROUND

This is where you explain the story so far. What research has been done on your area before and why did you feel the need to investigate? What is the context in which you are working? For example, some writers have likened studying Cold War defences to the study of prehistory, in that there are no accessible written or oral accounts available because of the requirements of the Official Secrets Act (see Schofield 2005 for example). If that is the case, what techniques from the study of prehistory can be applied and how are you using them? What is already known about your subject and what needs to be clarified? The important thing here is not to get carried away but to stick to a review of the relevant theories and information only.

METHODS

How did you go about gathering your evidence? Was it desk based or fieldwork, or both? This is what academics will be interested in. If they can pick holes, they will, but the point is that if the work is shown to be systematic, it will be sound. Even if it is wrong, it will show why your theory is wrong and narrow down the search for the next person. All research is valuable, provided it is based on a logical approach.

RESULTS

What evidence did you find? We have already considered a need for a study of the inter-relation of hillforts. This is the section in which you would discuss, for example, whether and in what conditions 'site A' is visible to 'site B'. It is also where the type of finds could be discussed. How much of what material was found where? What does that tell us? The absence of a particular calibre of ammunition may be even more significant than its presence. Are there items that should be there, but aren't?

DISCUSSION AND CONCLUSION

This is where you put forward your opinion of what you have found and what it tells us we didn't know before. It can be brief or it can be an opportunity to raise more questions than it answers, either is appropriate.

REFERENCES

To this, we also need to add a bibliography. Check this carefully. You need to ensure that readers are able to access the same information you have and that it is relevant to the content of the report. Different publications have different styles of referencing and will provide information on their preferred method. Look at how different authors have set out theirs and use them as a guide.

WRITING FOR PUBLICATION

Books

Having completed your research, you may want to consider publishing the results. The market for military history remains one of the most active in the publishing field but publishers are, after all, in business to make money. The first question will always be whether the book will sell and, regrettably, not all stories will.

Start by looking around bookshops and libraries for books like the one you want to produce. Check the market and where your book will fit in. List the publishers producing the type of book you want to write. Then, either by going online and searching or by consulting a copy of the Writers and Artists Yearbook in your local reference library, draw up a list of likely publishers.

In the first instance, a short letter will be enough to find out whether they feel your book is of interest. If so, they will write back to ask for further information. If not, they will save you the effort of sending a detailed description of something they will reject anyway. Remember when getting the inevitable first rejection that somewhere in the publishing world is a man who told J.K. Rowling that there was no market for books about a boy wizard. Editors who reject your work are clearly fools and you will get your own back at the awards ceremony.

In making a more formal approach, once a publisher has expressed some interest, you will need to prepare a proposal. Some publishers ask prospective writers to complete a questionnaire about themselves and their project, others will ask for a more general proposal but the basic information you will need to consider when putting together your ideas consists of:

1 An outline of the book's main argument, and why you think it should be published.
2 What you feel is the book's unique selling point ('USP'). This refers to what makes it different to any others that have been written on the subject and what new angle you are using to approach the subject. Describe how your book differs from the competition and note any special marketing points, e.g. anniversaries, exhibitions, to which your book relates. Mention any special or unique features of the book that they should consider and mention any possible areas of criticism.
3 The intended reader/audience for the book; mention any organisations or institutions making a study of your subject or list courses which may make the book required reading.
4 Tell them why you have written the book, and provide biographical information on yourself such as any academic credentials or anything that makes you an authority on the subject. Include the names of others in your field whom may be prepared to recommend your book.

The following material relating to the book should also be included:

A chapter-by-chapter synopsis (*c.*2–3 pages).

A table of contents.
The number of illustrations, colour or black and white.
The estimated length (word count) of the book.
An estimate of the date of completion of the work.

Some publishers prefer to see one or two sample chapters (the introduction being an ideal sample) but you should either check the website or write to request a copy of the author's guidelines for the company you select.

As an author, you may be expected to source any illustrations you use. You need to be aware of copyright use before contacting photo libraries and archives for permission to use their material (rates vary according to end use – international editions will be more expensive than UK-only rights for example).

You also need to be aware that it is a lengthy process – around nine to twelve months is typical. If your USP is linked to an anniversary, you need to factor this in to your writing schedule.

Magazines

If the material is not enough or you don't have time to write a book, magazines are an alternative. There are many history-based titles available and again, look around larger bookshops and magazine stores to find potential markets. Again, the Writers and Artists Yearbook offers advice and suggestions about writing and lists magazine who may accept your work.

The initial approach is similar to that of the book world – a quick letter or Email to the editor to test the waters. Be aware of the editor's needs. He or she is looking for someone who can produce the kind of material their readers want, in a style that fits with the rest of the magazine. Paid writing is obviously expected to be of high quality and if you're unsure or need to gain a bit of confidence, there are several magazines which don't have a budget to pay but who will perhaps offer a free subscription or something in return for material. These then help in approaches to other magazines who don't know you were not paid and assume that if you have been published before, you must be professional.

If you hope to gain any sort of reputation as a military historian, the work you do for books, magazines or even the local parish newsletter must be of high quality, presented well and on time. If you are sending pictures, make sure they are captioned clearly so that the editor knows what should go where and why. If you do that, you will (eventually) be published.

PHOTOGRAPHY

No matter how much they might appreciate photography or military history, a photo of an empty field is hardly going to grab anyone's attention. The problem is that on most battlefields today, that's all that there is to see, an empty field. Photography has an important part to play in battlefield archaeology as a record of the work undertaken, the finds recovered and in illustrating the story being pieced together. Yet, more often than not, it is added as an afterthought by writers who realise that they need something to support their text. A hundred years after Kodak advertised 'You push the button, we'll do the rest', there are many who still believe that that is all they have to do. Eric Houlder, an experienced archaeological site photographer has lamented falling standards in what is, after all, an essential element of the recording of any work, arguing that there are 'too few photographers who are archaeologists and too many archaeologists who imagine that they are also photographers!' (2006: 30). The main problem is a simple lack of thought about what is required.

Equipment

The most basic piece of equipment is obviously a camera. It is also the basis for the most annoying phrase any photographer can hear – the viewer who pipes up with 'that's a nice picture, you must have a good camera'. Imagine telling someone that you've enjoyed their cooking so 'you must have a good oven'. In fact, a camera is just a tool. It will not take great pictures, you will. The type of camera you use simply determines how much control you have over the results. There are a bewildering number of possible options, from digital cameras built into mobile phones to multi-thousand pound specialist imaging equipment. They all do the job, to different degrees. The cameras used to create some of the most famous images in history were crude in comparison to even some of the cheapest available today.

If you want to take more than simple snapshots, you will need a camera capable of allowing you to take control of the process. A simple point and shoot camera will not do that; although it's always useful to carry a camera of any kind for those unexpected finds where you need a quick reference shot. The arrival of high-quality digital cameras has increased the level of control in even the most basic cameras but for serious photography, a single lens reflex (SLR) camera is the best option. SLRs work by reflecting light through a mirror into the viewfinder so that, unlike other cameras where the viewfinder is offset to one side, the SLR viewfinder is directly above the lens and what you see in the viewfinder is what you will get in your shot. No more cutting off the tops of people's heads. It also allows more flexibility in dealing with different forms of light (see below).

Film SLRs are available cheaply and even cheaper on the second-hand market. As digital SLRs become more accessible, enthusiasts are trading in their old film equipment and prices are falling all the time. Reputable dealers will offer a three or even six-month guarantee with used equipment and can advise on what you need. A camera with spot metering (a facility that lets you adjust the exposure for a specific area of the shot) is especially useful for recording purposes. This facility is increasingly becoming standard on digital cameras of all types.

The film camera, though, is simply a lightproof box. It holds the film. The real work is done by the lens, and you need to budget for the best you can afford. Again, the second-hand market can offer some real bargains. SLRs allow you to remove and change the

66 British Second World War harbour defences, Port Stanley, Falkland Islands

type of lens according to the type of site you are working at. Inside a fortification, for example, a wide-angle lens (commonly around 18-35mm focal length) allows you to photograph a whole room in one shot, whilst a standard lens of a focal length of 50mm equates roughly to the field of view of the human eye. More often, though, you will find shops selling standard zooms. These are lenses of variable focal length (usually 28-70mm or 35-80mm) and offer more flexibility in acting as wide angle (useful for including large areas) or short telephoto (for isolating particular elements of a scene). Another option is the so-called 'superzoom', covering lengths from 28-300mm and capable of covering most eventualities. If possible, chose a lens with a 'macro' function. This allows you to move in close to your subject and is needed for recording small items 'in situ'. If you cannot afford something like that, or have a digital camera that doesn't allow you to change lenses, then look at the possibility of using macro filters. These are round pieces of glass that attach to the front of your existing lens and perform the same function.

The most common size for a film camera is 35mm (the size of film it is designed to take) but 'medium format' cameras are also widely used because of the greater quality of detail that the larger film size allows. Medium format is more expensive, heavier and complicated to use, so, unless you're very serious about your photography, you probably won't need to consider it. In either case, the type and quality of film will both affect the end result and, like with the lens, you should consider the best you can afford.

Digital cameras are another matter. Like film cameras, their intended use determines their quality, which is broadly indicated by their level of resolution measured in megapixels. The higher the number of megapixels, the better and clearer the picture will be. As a rough guide, the bottom end of the market, at 1.3M (megapixels) will deliver pictures comparable to film quality only at sizes of around 6'x4' (the smallest photographs produced by high street developers). To achieve larger prints and high quality images at around 8inx10in (or A4 paper size), around 5-6M are needed, whilst 8M can produce results equal to those from medium format film cameras and will print at sizes of A3, and even higher. If you are considering photographs for use in reports, articles or for display, a 6M digital SLR is ideal.

Whatever type of camera is used, one other purchase will be useful. A tripod will provide the camera with a steady platform and will slow you down enough to give you time to set up the shot more carefully.

Film versus digital

The popularity of digital cameras comes from their convenience and instant feedback. There's no more waiting to see what your shots are like, you can check them immediately – a great bonus where the light may be tricky and you need to make sure you have the shot you need. The initial outlay is expensive but once a memory stick has been bought, it can be used over and over, saving on processing costs. Gradually, film producers are reducing their output and it seems likely that within a few years the majority of photography will be digital. Until then, ordinary film remains popular and will always have its adherents.

Print

Print film is the type we are all familiar with. It can be processed within an hour in high street shops and comes back as a set of prints that can be conveniently left in the packet and lost down the back of a drawer. As with everything else in photography, it varies in quality and cost. The advantage is that you have a ready reference for sites and viewpoints that can be of enormous help in understanding a location but it also has disadvantages in terms of reproduction. Prints do not scan well for use in magazines and books and the costs involved in having professional copies made can be high.

Print film comes in either colour – the most popular and most easily available, or black and white (B&W). Colour, by virtue of being popular, is the easiest to have processed and is useful in showing changes in soil colour or other important site indicators. B&W is useful for more artistic images of sites and general recording. It's easier to process at home, but costly and slow to have done professionally. One option is to use B&W film specially designed for processing in the same way as colour – Ilford XP2 and Kodak both produce B&W films that use the same C41 process as ordinary colour films but may be printed as sepia tints due to the type of paper used by high street labs – you can always have them redone later, if you want genuine B&W. However, do not accept any suggestions that such films need special processing. Some high street labs may claim that such films have to be processed as B&W. They don't. That's the whole point. Don't allow them to try to charge extra for the service either. It's just ignorance on the part of the shop staff, but sadly all too common.

Slides

Slides, or transparencies, 'trannies' as they are also known, are also familiar from the dreaded holiday slide show. They can be cumbersome and difficult to store, but the images are better suited to reproduction than prints and generally preferred by most publishers. They also lend themselves to presentations and lectures in a way that prints do not. They are more difficult to use than print as the exposure needs to be more accurate. Print film can tolerate mistakes more easily than can slides.

Like print film, slide film can be bought in bulk from Channel Island retailers very cheaply and addresses are available from the photo press. Unlike print, slides also have the advantage that many can be bought 'process-paid'. Once the film is shot, it can be sent in the supplied envelope to a processor and returned as a box of developed and mounted images.

Speeds

Both print and slide films come in a variety of speeds measured as ASA (American Standards Association) or, more commonly, ISO (International Standards Organization) numbers. This relates to the level of sensitivity to light of the film and ranges, from slow films of ISO25 to fast films of ISO3200. Most widely available are films of 100, 200 and 400, although colour films of up to 1000 are becoming more easily obtainable. The numbers refer to the amount of light exposure they will need. An ISO 200 film will only need half the light of a 100, and so on.

In general, the slower the film, the more detailed it will be and the better it will reproduce. With that said, a compromise is needed between the quality of the shot and the amount of time it will take to produce. Recent improvements in film technology have meant that ISO 200 is now regarded as suitable for most purposes – fast enough to allow you to handhold the camera without blurring the shot through 'camera shake', but slow enough to produce clear detailed pictures.

Exposure

Linked to film speed, exposure is the amount of time the film is exposed to light. It is determined by two factors: shutter speed and aperture.

1 Shutter speed is measured in fractions of a second (1/125th, 1/250th, etc.). This, on many cameras, can be set by a dial on the body of the camera. Use it where the speed of the shutter is important – for freezing action, for example. It is also useful where 'camera shake' may be a problem. This occurs when handholding, the camera moves during the exposure, causing a blurring of the image. As a rule, if the shutter speed is greater than the focal length of the lens, then there should be no problem (e.g. a lens of 50mm can be hand held at 1/60th of a second).

2 Alternatively, the aperture can be used to control light. This is a ring on the lens marked from around f2.8 up to f22, or higher. This acts like the pupil of the eye – the

higher the number, the smaller the aperture. Wide apertures (the lower numbers) are useful in lower light but will reduce the 'depth of field' (the amount of the picture in focus). Where an object needs to be isolated from a cluttered background, a narrow depth of field will throw the background out of focus. A deeper depth of field, obtained by setting a higher number, will mean that everything from close to the camera to the far distance will be in focus.

These two factors work in tandem – the lower the aperture, the faster the shutter speed and vice versa. This allows you to decide which is more important to you at any given time.

If in doubt, photographers have the 'sunny f16 rule'. On a sunny day, set the aperture to f16 and the shutter speed to that nearest the film speed (e.g. 1/125th for an ISO100 film and so on). This should produce useable results and you can, with experience, begin to adjust the rule according to the weather.

Composition

The key to photography is simply to think about what the picture is for. If it is for recording a find, it will be a very different shot to one intended to show the site. Think about the shot and try to imagine how it will look. The human eye is many times more sensitive than even the best camera. So try half closing your eyes to get an idea of what will record and what may not. You will find that a lot of detail that seems visible will not be.

A simple recording shot can be set up easily, but again, think about why you are taking the shot. Does the object need to be in context or can it be equally useful to photograph it separately? Think about the best angle and don't simply snap away at what you can see from a standing position. By moving even a few feet, crouching or climbing on something, the picture may become far clearer. Move around first and make sure that you are able to include the relevant subjects and that they can be recognised – after all, a long shot of a camouflaged bunker won't be of much use if the camouflage is any good. At the same time, some sort of reference is going to be needed to show scale. Including a person or a car in the shot may help to give some idea of the size of an earthwork. At the other end of the scale, a matchbox, a coin or a ruler can be placed next to the artefact for the same reason.

In trying to illustrate a battlefield, you move more into the field of landscape photography and there are plenty of features in the amateur photography magazines to help. Again, it is a matter of thinking about what it is you are trying to show. In many cases there will be no obvious evidence of battle. If that is the case, then try to convey something of how the battlefield feels to you. Use 'foreground interest' – trees, flowers, fences or anything that you think gives a flavour of the area – to provide a focal point to your picture. Look at the sort of illustrations that you've seen in guidebooks. Often these are small details of houses or statues but say a lot about the region. That's the sort of thing you can use. Alternatively, if you have access to contemporary illustrations, a direct comparison shot of the type used so well by *After the Battle* magazine can work equally well.

Don't limit yourself to 'landscape' format shots because that is what you've always done. Try turning the camera on its side to take 'portrait' format too. Where possible, do both – it is useful for editors when arranging page layouts to have a choice. Experiment and look at other people's work to get new ideas. Part of the way you will be able to get support from others is by making your project look interesting.

Lighting

'Photography' actually means 'painting with light'. Without it, nothing will record on film. You need to think about the light available to you and how best to use it.

Early morning or late evening sunlight has what is referred to as a 'warm' cast to it. Everything takes on a reddish-gold tint that makes this a popular time of day with photographers who often refer to the 'golden hour'. This light comes from low down in the sky, when the smallest lumps and bumps become obvious. This is the perfect time to look for earthworks and trenches, and the time when they are most likely to record on film. It is also the time when shadows will be created and help define edges and cover. Be aware of sunrise and sunset times and make use of them.

Harsh, overhead sunshine will create problems for the photographer. The contrast levels are too high to record details, light areas will 'burn out' and become blobs of white or light grey and shaded areas will disappear into black. If there is no alternative to shooting between, roughly, 10 a.m. and 2 p.m., consider using 'fill flash' to help reduce contrast. The idea of using flash in strong sunlight seems a bit of a waste of time, but what it does is to fill in the areas that might otherwise be lost in shadow – again, half close your eyes and you'll immediately see that some parts of your shot will be unrecognisable unless you add some light. In the case of small areas, placing a piece of light-coloured card or cloth, or even an umbrella alongside the object, will bounce some light back to it and even things up a bit. However, if you are trying to record detail, then a bright but overcast day is ideal. The light is softer and more evenly spread and this allows the camera to record far more of the subtle changes in the subject.

Captioning

Unless you have a fantastic and infallible memory, take notes as you shoot. As you shoot a roll of film, give each roll a number and note each frame so that you can identify it later. If possible, photograph signs, plaques or any other identifying information at the same time to help track your shots. Each will need details of where, when and what they are. Put a reference number on every print or slide so that you can trace them if you need to. Digital cameras will do this automatically, but you still need to match the shot of 'empty field one' with the right caption because after a while, they all look alike.

If you plan to submit them for publication, include a caption sheet detailing the image number, what it is of and how it relates to your text. Always include enough to allow the editor a choice, but don't just send a pack of prints and leave them to get on with it.

Copyright and end use

Whenever you take a photograph, you have the copyright. That means no one can use the photo without your permission. You retain control of how and where the picture is used unless you sign away that right. If your photos are used by publishers, you licence that use (i.e. you give permission for them to use the shot for one time only) and may be entitled to some payment for it in some cases. Professional magazines rarely have much of a budget for such shots but some of the larger consumer magazines, those that accept advertising, may pay for use.

Most military histories will use contemporary illustrations obtained from picture libraries and museums. In these cases, the same principle applies. If you are using an illustration for your own use, you may find that permission will be given to use images either for free or for a minimal sum. Pictures used for publication, though, will have to be paid for. This is particularly an issue for the comparison shots mentioned above, since most original material will be stored in official archives.

One way around this is to begin to build a collection of your own. Flea markets, military fairs and attics are a great source of snapshots and postcards, especially from the First World War onwards. These can often be bought cheaply and come in useful for reference material. These are usually accredited to 'author's collection' when used in publications.

Photography should not be an 'add-on' to the project. It should be planned from the outset as another form of report and afforded a higher value than most professionals give it.

APPENDIX A

DEFENCE AND FORTIFICATION

Working in Durham, Dr David Petts has laid out a number of thematic strategies for the North East Regional Research Framework for the Historic Environment, part of which focuses on defence and fortification that demonstrates both the potential range and scope of military archaeology and the tremendous gaps in our existing understanding. The principles set out here can equally be applied in other areas.

The North East, perhaps more than any other region in Britain, has a long history of violence and conflict. From the Roman period onwards, it has been an important border zone and its east-facing coast has been seen as a vulnerable flank, open to attack from both elsewhere in Britain and across the North Sea. Whilst many of the individual threats have been period specific and contingent on the ebb and flow of political events, it is possible to identify a series of crosscutting research issues. This section aims to highlight some of these topics and put forward practical ways in which research into the defence and fortification of the north-east might be implemented.

FORTIFICATIONS: FUNCTION VERSUS SYMBOLISM

Traditional accounts of fortification, whether exploring Iron Age hillforts or medieval castles, have frequently been firmly functional, analysing them primarily as defensive structures, with any other symbolic or ideological functions being merely incidental. However, modern discussions of fortification are increasingly analysing the ideological impact of fortifications (e.g. Johnson 2002). Powerful defences can be symbols of domination, indicators of cohesive or divisive social identities, markers of corporate power or simply indications of high status. The construction of defensive structures cannot be analysed simply in terms of strategy and tactics.

Recommendations

There is a need to explore a range of fortification types, including hillforts, castles, medieval city walls and even Hadrian's Wall, to analyse their visual impact on their surrounding areas and to assess their visual impact on their hinterlands. Is there more investment in architecture on the main lines of approach than on other sides of the structure. Attention must also be given to stylistic elements of fortification, e.g. type of stone used … depiction of heraldic symbolism or marks of ownership.

There is a need for more detailed analysis of the setting of fortified sites. Do their locations indicate that aesthetic or symbolic considerations have been privileged over purely tactical matters? Do surrounding structures compromise the defensive integrity of the fortified structure? Is there evidence for parks, gardens or other elements of designed landscape in the curtilage of the fortification?

The above techniques should be explored using GIS (Geographical Information Systems) techniques to consider issues, such as intervisibility of sites, and the extent to which apparent networks of defensive structures really support each other tactically. There should also be increased internal analysis of the use of space and arrangement of rooms within castle structures (cf. Matthews 2000; Richards 2003).

A survey of the re-use of earlier sites by later defensives is needed. How many medieval castles re-use earlier Roman or Iron Age fortifications? Do their locations indicate functional or ideological adoption of these sites?

MILITARY TECHNOLOGY

Despite the requirement for detailed consideration of ideological and symbolic issues in analysing fortifications, there is a need for a more detailed consideration of the impact of changing military technology on the design and location of fortifications. However, the impact of new forms of military technology rely not just on scientific advances but also the chronology of the adoption of the new forms of weaponry. This is profoundly related to the changes in social aspects of warfare and the development of new tactics.

Recommendations

There is a need for more refined chronology of late architectural developments in the region's castles. How closely can these changes be related to the adoption of gunpowder? Is there any indication of defensive structures of varying status reacting to the increased use of guns and artillery at different times and in different areas?

What is the relationship between new forms of naval technology, ranging from the advent of steam power to the adoption of advances in naval artillery, including industrial production of ordnance, breech loading guns and rifling, to changing tactical approaches to coastal defence?

The recovery and analysis of any battle cemeteries should be made a priority. Detailed analysis of combat injuries will provide important information about mode of warfare.

COASTAL DEFENCE

The long eastern coast of the region has had a profound impact on the defence of the area. It has been seen variously as a potentially weak flank, an important means of communication and the main route for moving men and materiel. There is a need for close analysis of shifting tactical approaches to defending the coastline and sea lanes of the north-east.

Recommendations

Development of a GIS-based model of the coastline and inshore waters of the region, including details about major known navigational channels is needed. A detailed picture of shipping routes can be built up from existing charts, pilot manuals and the evidence from wrecks. This analytical model of the coastline could be used as base for exploring varying responses to perceived sea-based threats and how they relate to the technical capabilities of naval technologies. The recovery of naval vessels of the eighteenth century or earlier is a priority. The recovery and conservation of small arms and personal weapons from wreck assemblages is also of great importance.

There is a need for a conservation audit of coastal defences of all periods, particularly those in areas where there are high levels of coastal erosion.

BATTLEFIELDS AND SIEGE WORKS

The topic of battlefield archaeology has become increasingly recognised as a subject worthy of detailed research. There is a need to address the varying ways in which battlefields can be explored archaeologically, and ways in which the frequently ephemeral surviving remains of battlefields can be treated as a cultural heritage resource (Carman and Carman 2001).

RECOMMENDATIONS

There are currently six battlefields in the region recorded on the English Heritage Register of Historic Battlefields: Otterburn, Homildon Hill, Hallidon Hill, Newburn, Neville's Cross, and Flodden. These sites require the creation of a conservation plan and detailed research agenda.

The creation of a 'local list' of battle fields that might be important on a regional, rather than national, scale (e.g. Piperdean, Grindon, Carham, Hedgely Moor, Heavenfield) should be a priority.

There is a need for a pilot project, exploring all aspect of the archaeology of a major battlefield in the region. Flodden is a strong candidate for such a detailed survey.

An exploration of the afterlife of battlefields and their role as sites of commemoration and pilgrimage would make a strong MA dissertation.

There is a need for an audit of surviving English Civil War siege works and defensive structures. This should draw extensively on the excellent documentary resources.

'DEBATABLE LAND': FLUCTUATING BORDERS

Over much of the region's history, the land between the Tyne and Forth has been a border zone. This is a theme that can be found in the Roman period (Hadrian's Wall), the early medieval period (with the growth of the states of England and Scotland), the medieval period (Anglo-Scottish wars) and the post-medieval period (reiving and the '15 rebellion). There is a need to explore the various responses to fighting over, and living in these disputed territories. Topics of particular importance include if there was ever a 'borders' identity, the varying forms of conflict (state sponsored versus private initiative) and architectural responses to insecurity.

Recommendations

Peter Ryder has carried out an important survey of defensive structures in Northumberland. A similar project needs to be carried out in Durham. There is also need for a similar survey in southern Scotland. Only then can questions about the similarities and differences in 'reiver' society on both sides of the border be addressed.

A cross-period analysis of the location of fortified structures and battlefields should be carried out to assess the extent differences and similarities in strategic and tactical responses to warfare in the hostile upland landscape which characterises much of the landscape of the border zone.

How far did the Solway-Tyne line mark the southern edge of the border zone? To what extent were the North Pennines also a border zone? A survey of defensive structures in County Durham is an important element in exploring this question.

COMMUNICATION NETWORKS

All military forces require communication networks. These might leave no archaeological footprint, however, more permanent communication networks should leave more permanent remains

Recommendations

There is a need for detailed GIS modeling of networks of signal stations and beacons for all periods exploring the extent of intervisibility between known sites. There is scope for using this model as a predictive tool to locate gaps in the distribution of known sites. Such GIS-based modeling has particular potential for exploring the network of beacons established as a system to warn of border raids by reivers and the distribution of Roman signal stations up the east coast and across the Pennines via the Stainmore.

Comparisons should be made between the known routes of armies moving through the areas. To what extent is there consistency in the routes used by military forces heading both south and north? What factors influence the choices made about military movements?

'AN ARMY MARCHES ON ITS STOMACH': PROVISIONS AND LOGISTICS

There is a need to explore the varying responses taken to supplying military forces in the region. One useful approach would be the comparison between military forces supplied by states and those that are more 'embedded' in local society. There is a need to consider the role of armies as producers and consumers.

Recommendations

There is a need for full analysis of assemblages of faunal remains and plant macrofossils from military sites of all period, including Roman forts, medieval castles and post-medieval barracks.

Bibliography

Carman, J. and Carman P. 2001 Beyond military archaeology: Battlefields as a research resource. In P.W.M. Freeman and A. Pollard (eds) *Fields of Conflict: Progress and Prospects in Battlefield Archaeology*, Proceedings of a conference held in the Department of Archaeology, University of Glasgow, April 2000, BAR I 958, 275-81

Johnson, M. 2002 *Behind the Castle Gate: from the Middle Ages to the Renaissance*, Routledge

Matthews, J. 2000 New Methods on Old Castles: Generating New Ways of Seeing. *Medieval Archaeology* 43, 115-42

Richards, A. 2003 Gender and Space in English Royal Palaces c.1160-c.1547: A study in Access Analysis and Imagery. *Medieval Archaeology* 47, 131-65

© Dr David Petts. www.durham.gov.uk. *Used with permission*

APPENDIX B
NATO MAP SYMBOLS

(BASED ON NATO APP-6 MANUAL)

Major Tom Mouat MBE has produced an excellent resource for anyone seeking to understand the use of military map symbols, including a free downloadable font to allow users to use the symbols in documents (www.mapsymbs.com).

Below are the basic military symbols likely to be encountered in accounts of military action. Allied units are coloured blue or have a single line outline. Enemy forces are marked in red or have a double outline.

BASIC UNITS

☐ This is the basic friendly unit symbol. The location is the centre of the bottom line

☐ This is the Headquarters symbol for a unit. The location is at the base of the longer line

☐ This is the basic enemy unit symbol if not in colour

BASIC UNIT INDICATORS

⊠	▱	⊡
Infantry	Reconnaissance (also used for mounted cavalry)	Artillery

▢	▢	▢
Armoured	Parachute	Engineers

These symbols can be combined with other symbols to denote specialist units e.g.:

⊠ Mechanized Infantry

⊠ Airborne Engineers

⊠ Enemy Artillery Locating Unit

UNIT SIZE INDICATORS

⊠ Smallest unit (half section of 4 men)
⊠ Section
⊠ Platoon
⊠ Company or Squadron
⊠ Battalion
⊠ Regiment

⊠ Brigade
⊠ Division
⊠ Corps
⊠ Army
⊠ Army Group

WEAPONS SYMBOLS

| ↑ ╪ ╪

Rifle   Machine guns (the addition of lines denotes light to heavy)

╟ ╫ ╫

Gun or howitzer (again, light to heavy types)

⥮   ●

Mortar   Land mine

APPENDIX C
RESOURCES

GETTING STARTED

There are plenty of books available to help understand the theory and practice of archaeology and fieldwork. Below are some of the easiest entry points into what can be an incredibly complex subject:

ARCHAEOLOGY

Clive Gamble's *Archaeology – The basics* (Routledge 2004) is an easy to read introduction to the theories and concepts of archaeology in general and provides a useful primer to the discipline.

Anthony Brown's *Fieldwork for Archaeologists and Local Historians* (Batsford 1987), is an indispensable starting point for fieldwork surveys – a clearly written guide to desk-based research, maps and fieldwork. It is the ideal reference work for the study of landscapes.

Tony Robinson and Professor Mick Aston are familiar to viewers of the television programme *Time Team* which, over the past decade, has probably been the inspiration behind thousands of applications to study archaeology. Their book *Archaeology is Rubbish* (Channel 4 Books 2002) is a step by step guide to conducting your own mini-excavation.

Battlefield archaeology
Tony Pollard and Neil Oliver have done much to popularise battlefield archaeology in Britain with their television series *Two Men in a Trench*. Two books accompanying the series describe the theory and practice of battlefield research at a number of sites around Britain (Michael Joseph Books).

Battlefield Detectives by David Wason (Granada Books 2003) accompanies the television series of the same name and describes how archaeology, metal detecting and forensic science are adding to our understanding of battlefields.

Earl Swift's *Where They Lay* (Bantam Press 2003) is an account of his experiences with a specialist military recovery team on an expedition to Laos searching for the remains of US aircrew still listed as missing in action.

Richard Osgood's *The Unknown Warrior: An Archaeology of the Common Soldier* (Sutton Publishing 2005) is an exploration of the recovery of combat casualty remains from battlefields across history.

Phillippe Planel's *A Teacher's Guide to Battlefields, Defence, Conflict and Warfare* (English Heritage 1995) is both a useful introduction to the field of conflict study and an opportunity to prove that it's not just about you, it's good for the kids too. Other EH guides include *A Teacher's Guide to Using Castles* (T. Copeland 1994) and *A Teacher's Guide to Using Memorials* (S. Purkis 1995).

Military history

Long the preserve of retired officers, military histories have often tended towards being impenetrable for the novice reader. There is, however, a trend towards a more readable approach that has resulted in a number of excellent studies reaching the bestseller lists. There are too many books that will reward the effort of finding to list here but a few are worth mentioning as a good starting point.

Professor Richard Holmes is perhaps one of the best known military historians and any of his books are highly recommended. In particular, his *War Walks* books, written to accompany the television series of the same name (published as separate books in 1996 and 1997 and as a compendium in 2003 by BBC Books), are an example of how such accounts should be told. His *Riding the Retreat* (Pimlico 1995) is part travelogue and part history as he describes a journey along the route of the 1914 Mons retreat – Battlefield tourism at its best.

The Osprey publishing company continues to produce well illustrated and easily available books on a wide range of military subjects, ranging from its *Men at Arms* series of uniform and equipment guides, to its *Campaign* series, describing particular actions. However obscure the period you wish to study, chances are that Osprey will have something for you.

GROUPS AND SOCIETIES

The upsurge in interest in archaeology in general means that there are more opportunities than ever to study the subject but, at the same time, fewer and fewer job openings for professional posts. More fieldwork is being undertaken by amateur groups on a voluntary basis as funding becomes evermore scarce. The good news is that this shift away from archaeology as an isolated, remote discipline and towards an era of public archaeology has brought with it an awareness of the need to involve members of the public at every level. The Council for British Archaeology produces an annual listing of current work, volunteer societies and training which could allow you the opportunity to develop skills and experience.

Council for British Archaeology (CBA)

The CBA is the central body for archaeology and provides advice and information on training, fieldwork opportunities, grants and awards, a nationwide network of childrens' archaeology groups and more. It publishes two magazines: *Current Archaeology* and *Current World Archaeology*, both widely available in bookstores and newsagents. It also publishes an annual *Current Archaeology Handbook*, which lists groups and upcoming projects.

> The Council for British Archaeology
> St Mary's House
> 66 Bootham
> York
> YO30 7BZ
> Tel: 01904 671417
> Email: info@britarch.ac.uk
> Website: www.britarch.ac.uk

National Council for Metal Detecting (NCMD)

The NCMD provides a forum for metal detectorists and has been working closely with professional battlefield archaeologists to develop codes of practice to enable the two bodies to work together. Details are available from:

> General Secretary,
> NCMD
> 51 Hilltop Gardens
> Denaby
> Doncaster
> DN12 4SA
> Tel: 01709 868521
> Email: Trevor.austin@ncmd.co.uk
> Website: www.mcmd.co.uk

Conflict Archaeology International Research Network (CAIRN)

A web-based network of professional researchers sharing information on current events and trends in battlefield studies. Although primarily for professionals, it is also an excellent source of advice and information to anyone with an interest in conflict studies (www.cairnworld.free.fr).

The Battlefields Trust

The Battlefields Trust is a charitable body set up to protect battlefield sites in the UK. It actively supports members in researching Britain's military history. Its co-ordinator, Michael Rayner, has written *English Battlefields* (Tempus 2004), a guide to over 500 known battle sites in Britain. As the author freely admits, the list is not exhaustive. For more information contact:

The Battlefields Trust
Meadow Cottage,
33 High Green,
Brooke,
Norwich,
NR15 1HR
Phone/Fax: 01508 558145
Email: national.coordinator@battlefieldstrust.com
Website: www.battlefieldstrust.com

The trust also runs a national resource centre which was under the guidance of Glenn Foard, a name familiar to anyone with an interest in battlefield archaeology.
Email: project.officer@battlefieldstrust.com

English Heritage

English Heritage is the government's statutory advisory body on heritage conservation issues and actively promotes awareness of Britain's history. Members enjoy free access to properties maintained by English Heritage and to a number of events around the country, ranging from lectures and tours to re-enactment shows. It also maintains a database (the National Monuments Record) of some 10 million items, including aerial photographs, archaeological records and drawings and plans of buildings. Many of these are available for free consultation and there is an active outreach programme of evening classes, guided tours and workshops open to the public. There is also a landscape archaeology department which offers advice and information.

General enquiries and membership:

Customer Services Department
PO Box 569
Swindon
SN2 2YP
Tel: 0870 333 1181
Email: customers@english-heritage.org.uk
Website: www.english-heritage.org.uk

National Monuments Record:

NMR Enquiry and Research Services
English Heritage
National Monuments Record Centre
Swindon
SN2 2GZ
Tel: 01793 414600

Email: nmrinfo@english-heritage.org.uk
Website: www.english-heritage.org.uk

Elsewhere, Historic Scotland perform a similar function:

Friends of Historic Scotland
Longmore House
Salisbury Place
Edinburgh
EH9 1SH
Tel: 0131 668 8999
Email: hs.friends@scotland.gsi.gov.uk
Website: www.historic-scotland.gov.uk

And in Wales:

Cadw
Welsh Assembly Government
Plas Carew
Unit 5/7 Cefn Coed
Parc Nantgarw
Cardiff
CF15 7QQ
Tel: 01443 33 6000
Fax: 01443 33 6001
Email: Cadw@Wales.gsi.gov.uk
Website: www.cadw.wales.gov.uk

Ordnance Survey
Customer Service Centre
Ordnance Survey
Romsey Road
Southampton
SO16 4GU
Email: customerservices@ordnancesurvey.co.uk
Tel: (general enquiries) 08456 05 05 05

Reprints of old OS maps can be downloaded from:
www.old-maps.co.uk
www.british-history.ac.uk

RE-ENACTMENT GROUPS

National Association of Re-enactment Societies
    Des Thomas
    Secretary N. A. Re. S.
    Alma House,
    72 Cow Close Road,
    Leeds
    LS12 5PD
    Tel 0113 229 6759
    Fax 0113 229 6760
    Email: des1622@ntlworld.com
    Website: www.nares.org.uk

Call to Arms
Annual directory of re-enactment groups and services:

    Call to Arms sales
    1 Lyng Lane
    North Lopham
    Norfolk IP22 2HR
    Tel: 0870 789 8778

Skirmish Magazine
Re-enactment news and events:

    Dane Mill Business Centre
    Broadhurst Lane
    Congleton
    Cheshire
    CW12 1LA
    Tel: 01260 291536
    Email: Rachel@skirmishmagazine.co.uk
    Website: www.skirmishmagazine.co.uk

Living History
A multi-period forum with links to just about everything you might need to know about the world of re-enacting (www.livinghistory.co.uk).

STUDY GROUPS

These are general groups covering a range of periods. Other groups are listed by period below:

Arms and Armour Society
PO Box 10232
London
SW19 2ZD
Tel: 01323 844278
Email: Edmund@jbgreenwood.force9.co.uk
Website: www.armsandarmour.net

Castle Studies Group
Mylnmede
Moor Lane
Potterhanworth
Lincoln
LN4 2DZ
Tel: 01522 792780
Email: Pamelamarshall@mylnmede.freeserve.co.uk
Website: www.castlestudiesgroup.org.uk

Fortress Study Group
6 Lanark Place
London
W9 1PS
Tel: 020 7286 5512
Email: billandliz.clements@btinternet.com

Ordnance Society
3 Maskell Way
Southwood
Farnborough
GU14 0PU
Tel: 01252 521201
Email: ordnance.society@virgin.net
Website: www.freespace.virgin.net/ordnance.society//index.htm

Society for Landscape Studies
c/o Mrs K Brown
38 Mill Road, Bozeat
NN29 7JA

Email: Kathryn.s.brown@tesco.net
Website: www.landscapestudies.com

UK Forts Club
4 Maplethorpe Road
Wymering
Portsmouth
PO6 3LJ
Tel: 023 9238 7794
Email: peter@forthunter.freeserve.co.uk
Website: www.mysite.freeserve.com/ukfc/

UK National Inventory of War Memorials
Imperial War Museum
Lambeth Road
London
SE1 6HZ
Tel: 020 7207 9863
Email: memorials@iwm.org.uk
Website: www.iwm.org.uk

BY PERIOD

Prehistoric

The earliest recorded invasion of Britain was that of the Celts around 700 BC, arriving from France. Prior to the Roman invasion of Britain, however, we have no written accounts of British life and so the period is literally prehistoric.

Books

Dyer, James *Hillforts of England and Wales* (revised edition 2003) Shire Archaeology Series No. 16)

Williams, Geoffrey *Stronghold Britain: Four Thousand Years of British Fortification* (Sutton Publishing 1999)

Groups/Societies

Experimental Earthworks Committee
North Farm
West Overton
Marlborough
Wiltshire
SN8 1QE

Tel: 01672 861689
Email: grswanton@aol.com

The Hillfort Study Group
The Straddle Barn
Cholderton
Salisbury
Wiltshire
SP4 0DW
Tel: 01980 629210
Email: cynbyn@tesco.net

Re-enactment groups

Brigantia
67 Paulsgrove Road
North End
Portsmouth
Hants
PO2 7HP
Tel: 023 9269 6897
Email: secretary@lugoduc.demon.co.uk
Website: www.ironage.demon.co.uk/brigantia

Bronze Age Re-enactment
11 Linden Grove
Hayling Island
Hampshire
PO11 9DG
Tel: 07970 614330
Email: info@bronze-age-reenactment.com
Website: www.bronze-age-reenactment.com

Silures Iron Age Society
25 Anchorsholme Lane East
Thornton Cleveleys
Lancashire
FY5 3QH
Tel: 01253 852235
Email: heather.holt@silures.fsnet.co.uk

Roman

Julius Caesar launched a large-scale raid into Britain in 54 BC, but it was not until AD 43 that Roman military power was brought to bear to bring the country into the Roman Empire under the command of Aulus Plauticus for the Emperor Claudius.

Books
Webster, G. *The Roman Invasion of Britain* (London 1993)

Williams, Geoffrey *Stronghold Britain: Four Thousand Years of British Fortification* (Sutton Publishing 1999)

Groups/societies
Association for Roman Archaeology
75 York Road
Swindon
Wiltshire
SN1 2JU
Tel: 01793 534008
Email: ara.zarriba@zyworld.com
Website: www.zyworld.com/zarriba/ara.htm

Britannia: Aspects of the Roman Army in Britain
7 Prospect Hill
Old Town
Swindon
SN1 3JU
Email: Britannia@morgue.demon.co.uk
Website: www.morgue.demon.co.uk

Roman Military Research Society
190 Lightwoods Road
Smethwick
West Midlands
B67 5AZ
Email: peters.noons@btconnect.com
Website: www.romanArmy.net

Re-enactors
Cohors V. Gallorum
Arbeia Roman Fort
Baring Street
South Shields
NE33 2BB
Tel: 0191 454 4093

Ermine Street Guard
Oakland Farm
Dog Lane
Witcombe
Gloucestershire
GL3 4UG
Tel: 01452 862235
Email: theesg@aol.com
Website: www.esg.ndirect.co.uk

Dark ages and the Norman Conquest

Between the departure of the Romans in AD 410 and the arrival of the Normans in 1066, Britain entered the Dark Ages. It was a time of struggle between competing invaders, Saxons, Angles and, of course, Vikings. A number of fortified towns arose during this period, leaving the place name 'burgh' on maps across the country. The Norman conquest of Britain in 1066 then sparked an unprecedented surge in castle building and few areas were not controlled by some sort of Norman fortification.

Books

Anglo-Saxon Chronicles

Williams, Geoffrey *Stronghold Britain: Four Thousand Years of British Fortification* (Sutton Publishing 1999)

Re-enactors

Dark Ages Society
Flat 5
350 Stapleton Road
Eastville
Bristol
BS5 0NN
Email: zoefly@blueyonder.co.uk
Website: www.darkagessociety.org

Regia Anglorum
9 Durleigh Close
Headley Park
Bristol
BS13 7NQ
Tel: 0117 9646818
Email: webmaster@regia.org
Website: www.regia.org

The Vikings
19 Boundary Road
Laverstock
Salisbury
SP1 1RN
Tel: 01722 504775
Website: www.vikingsonline.org.uk

Medieval

As Britain accepted its Norman conquerors, a new royal dynasty was established. Powerful families vied for control of the state and a series of civil wars, and rebellions over the next centuries would lead to the consolidation of the Norman fortifications and the development of new styles of building to counter the new threat – artillery.

Books

Cruickshank, Dan *Invasion* (Boxtree 2001)

Brown, R.A. *English Medieval Castles* (Batsford 1954)

Re-enactors

The Medieval Siege Society
www.medieval-siege-society.co.uk

Medieval Combat Society
www.montacute.net or www.themcs.org

Websites

The Internet Medieval Sourcebook is a site covering just about everything you will need to know about the period (www.fordham.edu/halsall/sbook.html).

The Richard III Society provides a good introduction to the troubled king and the background to the civil war that brought his reign to an end (www.richardiii.com).

ECW

The English Civil War is generally regarded as having taken place between 1642 and 1645. The period we most often associate with the Civil War was just one of a series of clashes between 1639 and 1651, when the war was finally be said to be over.

Books

Harrington, Peter *English Civil war Archaeology* (Batsford 2004) and *English Civil War Fortifications 1642-1651* (Osprey 2003)
Roberts, I. *Pontefract Castle: The Archaeology of the Civil War* (West Yorkshire Archaeology Service 1988)

Re-enactors

English Civil War Society
70 Hailgate
Howden
DN14 7ST

The King's Army
KA@english-civil-war-society.org

The Roundhead Association
RA@english-civil-war-society.org
Website: www.english-civil-war-society.org/

Sealed Knot
The Sealed Knot Ltd
Burlington House
Botleigh Grange Business Park
Southampton Hampshire
SO30 2DF
Email: info@sealedknot.org
Website: www.sealedknot.org/

Eighteenth and nineteenth century

Throughout the eighteenth and nineteenth centuries, fortification and military defence continued to be a major issue. In the wake of the '45 rebellion, a military presence was considered essential to control the population. Later, the threat of a Napoleonic invasion led to the creation of a network of towers, castles, roads and canals across southern England to counter the expected attack. Even as late at the mid-nineteenth century, 'Palmerston's Follies', a series of strong coastal fortifications were being built.

Fort George

Built in the wake of the battle of Culloden, Fort George was built to defend against any future Jacobite unrest. The result was the mightiest artillery fortification in Britain, if not Europe. Today it combines a museum with a working military barracks.

Fort George is located 10km west of Nairn, 18km north-east of Inverness off the A96. Its grid reference is NH 762 567. It is open all year, except on 25 & 26 December. It is open on 1 & 2 January – please telephone nearer the time for opening hours. In the summer, it is open 1 April to 30 September, Monday to Sunday 9.30 a.m. to 6.30 p.m.. In the winter it is open 1 October to 31 March, Monday to Sunday 9.30 a.m. to 4.30 p.m. The last tickets are sold at 5.45 p.m. (3.45 p.m. in winter). Tel 01667 460232

Fort Paull

A Napoleonic era fortress on the banks of the Humber, Fort Paull stands on the site of an earlier Henrican castle.

> Fort Paull Museum
> Battery Road
> Paull nr. Kingston Upon Hull
> East Yorkshire
> HU12 8FP
> Fort Paull (Tel): 01482 896236
> Head Office (Tel): 01482 882655
> Events manager (Tel): 01482 813010
> Website: www.fortpaull.com
> Open 10.00 till 18.00 British summer, 11.00 till 16.00 winter

Martello Towers

Alongside these forts, a string of fortified towers were built along the South coast. Its website is dedicated to their history and preservation (www.martello-towers.co.uk).

Books

Clements, W.H. (1999) *Towers of Strength – The Story of the Martello Towers.* Barnsley: Leo Cooper

Telling, R.M., PhD CEng (1997) *English Martello Towers – A Concise Guide.* Beckenham: CST Books

Telling, R.M., PhD CEng (1998) *Handbook on Martello Towers.* Beckenham: CST Books

> Palmerston Forts Society
> 17 Northcroft Road
> Gosport
> Hants
> PO12 3DR
> Tel: 023 9258 6575
> Email: webmaster@palmerstonforts.org.uk
> Website: www.palmerstonforts.org.uk

First World War

The Great War left its scars across Europe and beyond. There are thousands of memorials to those who died in towns, villages, workplaces and schools across Britain.

Neil Oliver's *Not Forgotten* (Hodder& Stoughton 2005) tells the stories of some of those commemorated.

Pen & Sword Books have produced a series of battlefield guides to the Western Front and another series of histories of the Pals Battalions, all well worth reading.

The best starting point for any study of the war has to be:

Western Front Association
PO Box 1918
Stockport
SK4 4WN
Tel: 0161 443 1918
Website: www.westernfrontassociation.com

The association offers members access to lectures, research materials and tours, as well as having links with other organisations. Three other essential sites are:

www.firstworldwar.bham.ac.uk – the University of Birmingham's Centre for First World War Studies
www.firstworldwar.com – an exceptional site covering a huge range of topics related to the war
www.1914-1918.net – The Long-Long Trail is and ever expanding mine of information

Re-enactment

There are many groups recreating the First World War and the Great War Society acts as an umbrella organization for many of them (www.thegreatwarsociety.com).

Second World War and Cold War
Osborne, Mike *Defending Britain: 20th Century Military Structures in the Landscape* (Tempus 2004)

Willis, H. *Pillboxes: A Study of UK Defences 1940* (Leo Cooper 1985)

Lowry, B. *20th Century Defences in Britain: An Introductory Guide* (Council for British Archaeology 1996)

Winton, Helen, Newsome, Sarah & Hegarty Cain. The Greatest Battlefield that Never Was. In Jon Cooksey (ed.) *Battlefields Annual Review* (Pen & Sword 2005)

Defence of Britain Project database (www.britarch.ac.uk)

Pillbox Study Group
3 Chelwood Drive, Taunton
Somerset, TA1 4JA

Tel: 07970174 715
Email: Fortress2000@hotmail.com
Website: www.pillbox-study-group.org.uk

Re-enactment

The Second World War is one of the most popular periods for re-enactment. Groups have been formed covering a wide range of units, from the Women's Land Army to the SAS. The WWII Living History Association is one of the larger umbrella groups:

WWII LHA
25 Olde Farm Drive
Darby Green
Camberley
Surrey
GU17 0DU

AVIATION

Bédoyère, Guy de la *Aviation Archaeology in Britain* (Shire Archaeology Series No. 80, Shire Books 2001)

Neil Oliver and Tony Pollard have written about their work at RAF Hornchurch in *Two Men in a Trench Vol II* (Michael Joseph Books 2003)

Airfield Research Group
33a Earls Street
Thetford
Norfolk
IP24 2AB
Tel: 01842 765399
Email: Ray.Towler@btinternet.com
Website: www.airfield-research-group.co.uk

Imperial War Museum Duxford
Cambridgeshire
CB2 4QR
Tel: 01223 835 000
Fax: 01223 837 267
Email: duxford@iwm.org.uk
Houses the IWM's aviation collection and its collection of armoured fighting vehicles.

NAVAL

Nautical Archaeology Society
Fort Cumberland
Fort Cumberland Road
Eastney
PO4 9LD
Tel: 023 9281 8419
Email: nas@nasportsmouth.org.uk
Website: www.nasportsmouth.org.uk

Historical Maritime Society (HMS)
Chris Jones
2 Mount Zion
Brownbirks Street, Cornholme
Todmorden
Lancashire OL14 8PG
Tel: 01706 819248 or 07850 947977
Email: grog@tesco.net
Website: www.hms.org.uk

HMS Belfast
Morgan's Lane
Tooley Street
London SE1 2JH
Tel: 0207 940 6300
Fax: 0207 403 0719
Email: hmsbelfast@iwm.org.uk

PUBLISHERS

Pen and Sword Ltd is a specialist publisher producing military histories, including the
Battleground Europe guides to the First World War and to battlesites around Europe. These
guides can be invaluable when attempting to trace an action on the ground today. For
details of the titles available contact:

Pen & Sword Books Ltd
47 Church Street
Barnsley
South Yorkshire
S70 2AS
Tel: 01226 734555

Email: enquiries@pen-and-sword.co.uk
Website: www.pen-and-sword.co.uk

Wharncliffe Books, an imprint of Pen and Sword, specialises in local history titles and can also be contacted at the above address.

Osprey Books produce several series of books, including:

Osprey Fortress: Each examining different types of fortification systems from ancient castles to First World War trench systems.
Osprey Men-At-Arms: Reference works covering the uniforms and equipment of hting soldiers throughout history.
Osprey Campaign: Accounts of specific encounters providing an easily accessible starting point for understanding a battle or a campaign
Essential Histories: Brief but detailed histories of major campaigns and wars.

Contact:
　Osprey Direct
　PO Box 140
　Wellingborough
　Northants NN8 2FAUK
　Tel: 01933 443 863
　Email: info@ospreydirect.co.uk
　Website: www.ospreypublishing.com

The Naval & Military Press offers reprints of out of print histories, training manuals and biographies. Its catalogue is a goldmine for researchers – everything from a complete muster roll of all recipients of the Military General Service Medal between 1793 and 1814 to a twenty-volume history of the British Army, from a supplier which offers 'Specialised Books for the Serious Student of Conflict'. No argument here.

　The Naval & Military Press Ltd
　Unit 10
　Ridgewood Industrial Park
　Uckfield
　East Sussex
　TN22 5QE
　Tel: 01825 749494
　Email: order.dept@nmpbooks.com
　Website: www.naval-military-press.com

MUSEUMS AND ARCHIVES

Imperial War Museum (IWM)

The IWM operates a number of museums dealing with twentieth-century warfare across the country from its headquarters in London. It has extensive documentary and photographic collections available for use.

> Imperial War Museum London (Headquarters)
> Lambeth Road
> London SE1 6HZ
> United Kingdom
> Tel: 020 7416 5320
> Fax: 020 7416 5374
> Email: mail@iwm.org.uk

> Imperial War Museum North
> The Quays
> Trafford Wharf
> Trafford Park
> Manchester M17 1TE
> Tel: 0161 836 4000
> Fax: 0161 836 4012
> Email: iwmnorth@iwm.org.uk

National Army Museum

The history of the British Army and venue for a number of battlefield archaeology exhibitions and lectures.

> National Army Museum
> Royal Hospital Road
> Chelsea
> London
> SW3 4HT
> Information Line: 020 7881 2455
> Email: info@national-Army-museum.ac.uk
> Tel: 020 7730 0717 (switchboard)

Royal Armouries

The main museum of the Royal Armouries is based at:
> Royal Armouries Museum
> Armouries Drive
> Leeds
> West Yorkshire LS10 1LT

The artillery collection is housed in:

> Royal Armouries Fort Nelson
> Portsdown Hill Road
> Fareham
> Hampshire
> PO17 6AN

The National Archives

The National Archives, formerly known as the Public Record Office, is the main depository for historic documentation and holds official reports, war diaries and many other items of use to the researcher. It also holds information on professional researchers able to undertake work on your behalf – expensive, but potentially more useful than trying to work long distance. Contact:

> The National Archives
> Kew
> Richmond
> Surrey
> TW9 4DU.
> Tel: 020 8876 3444
> Website: www.nationalarchives.gov.uk

The Access to Archives (A2A) website is an invaluable resource allowing you to search local archives and save hours of wasted time traveling to visit libraries around the country (www.a2a.org.uk).

The Ogilby Trust provides details of military museums around the country. Contact:

> Brigadier C.S. Sibun
> Army Museums Ogilby Trust
> 58 The Close
> Salisbury
> Wiltshire SP1 2EX
> Tel/Fax: 01722 332188
> Email: dir@amot.demon.co.uk
> Website: www.Armymuseums.org.uk

GLOSSARY

Abatis	Obstacles such as felled trees placed on the glacis of a work to break up an attack.
Approaches	Siegeworks. Trenches dug towards fortifications to allow the attackers to get in close before the final assault.
Bailey	Originally the courtyard of a fortified motte, the term is now applied to the courtyard of any castle.
Banquette	The firestep behind the parapet of a fire trench.
Barbican	A defensive work set out in advance of the main fortifications to protect the gates of a town or castle or approaches to bridges.
Bastion	A work comprised of two faces and two flanks which form part of a larger work. They are joined by curtains and sited so that the whole escarp can be brought under fire.
Berm	The space between the top of the escarp and the base of the ramparts as a communication path and to stop debris from filling the ditch.
Blockhouse	Originally a small detached fort used to protect a strategic point, the term is loosely applied to any standing position able to withstand attack.
Breach	A gap in defences caused by an attack.
Breastwork	See Parapet.
Bunker	Originally used to refer to a protected position for troops to live in, it has become associated with any underground position.
Casemate	Originally a chamber within the ramparts of a fortification from which artillery can be fired from cover. Now applied to fixed protected artillery positions such as those built by the Germans along the Atlantic Wall.
Citadel	A fortification within a town, usually sited on high ground and dominating both the town itself and the surrounding countryside. It forms the last line of defence for the town's garrison.
Command	The building of defence works so that they are able to dominate an area by their height and fields of fire.
Communication Trench	Also referred to as 'CT', a logistics trench built to connect the front-line trenches with the rear areas. Usually running at right angles to the front line.
Counterscarp	The vertical outer wall of the ditch around a fortification on the enemy's side. Much less vulnerable to fire than the scarp, which faces the enemy.
Cupola	An armoured dome to protect guns or other equipment mounted underneath.
Curtain	The main wall of a castle between turrets.

Deep Dugout	The British equivalent of the German *Hangstellung*, an underground dormitory. In the First World War, these could include railway and canal tunnels.
Defence in depth	The principle of having several layers of defence rather than relying on a single line.
Ditch	The excavation in front of a rampart. The soil from the ditch is used to build the earthworks supporting the ramparts. The ditch may be left dry or filled with water to act as a moat.
Dugout	Any underground space with cover for troops to live in.
Embrasure	An opening in a parapet or wall through which a weapon can be fired.
Enfilade	Fire directed from the side along a line so that missiles will have the maximum effect. In early trenches, dug in straight lines, any attacker able to take part of the trench could then simply fire along its length in both directions. Similarly, an artillery shell could spread shrapnel and splinters more widely as the trench channelled the blast. The use of traverses prevents this.
Escalade	An assault on walls using ladders.
Escarp	The inner wall of a ditch, facing the enemy.
Esplanade	The open space between a citadel and the town.
Feste	(German: 'stronghold') a First World War term for a defensive locality using dispersed positions rather than a single fortress.
Field of fire	The area over which a weapon can be brought to bear. Positions should be sited to ensure that weapons can be used to support each other by overlapping their fields of fire.
Fieldworks	Temporary fortifications usually built by the attackers.
Flying Sap	A sap dug in a single night so that the enemy is unaware of it.
Fort	Position or building designed for defence.
Fortress	Larger version of a fort, often encompassing a whole town and capable of holding a large force.
Fougasse	A hole in the ground filled with explosive covered by stones, metal or even fuel that can be detonated by troops under attack as a kind of giant shotgun. Widely used at roadblocks by the Home Guard of the Second World War.
Gabion	A cylinder of brushwood, wire netting or similar filled with earth to reinforce the sides of fieldworks.
GIS	Geographical Information Systems. A computer programme which allows finds to be accurately plotted and enables, for example, the intervisibility of sites to be determined. One advantage being that from existing data, it is able to predict other likely locations for sites.
GPS	Global Positioning System. A handheld system that communicates with US military satellites to give a pinpoint location on the ground.
Glacis	The area on the enemy side of the ditch that slopes down into the ditch. The enemy must cross this space under fire in order to attack.
Gorge	The back wall of a fortress, facing away from the enemy.
Henrican Fort	One of the fortifications built during the reign of Henry VIII to counter French and Spanish threats.
Keep	Generally referring to the main building of a medieval castle. The keep is taken as meaning the centre of a defence work.
Mine	Traditionally a tunnel dug under the walls of a castle. Once underneath the walls, a fire could be started to burn out the timbers shoring up the mine causing it to collapse. This in turn would cause the walls above to fall. Later, gunpowder was used and, in the First World War, huge quantities of explosives were placed under the enemy trenches and detonated. The later development of the land mine is really a very localised version of the same principle.
Moat	Common term for ditch. See motte.
Motte	The mound topped by a palisade forming the basis of a Norman castle. Artificial

mounds were created by the digging of a ditch – hence the term 'motte' became associated with the ditch and has evolved into moat.

Pallisade	A row of closely placed sharpened stakes. Can refer either to the wooden walls of a fort or to obstacles on the glacis.
Palmerston Fort	Part of a series of forts built in the mid-nineteenth century under Lord Palmerston and often referred to as 'Palmerston's Follies'.
Parallel	Trench dug by besieging force parallel to the defences so that the attackers could be brought as close as possible to the target for the final assault.
Parados	The raised bank to the rear of a trench to protect from artillery falling behind the line.
Parapet	The bank on the enemy side of a trench over which the defenders are able to fire. Also sometimes known as a breastwork.
Pillbox	A concrete structure built above ground to house infantry and machine guns. So called as they resembled the small decorative boxes used to store medicines.
Rampart	A bank built behind the ditch to enable defenders to command the approaches.
Ravelin	Triangular detached work in the ditch to break up an attack.
Redan	An arrow shaped protrusion from a wall.
Redoubt	A small, independent work, usually square and entirely surrounded by a parapet. Redoubts were used in the Crimea to command hill tops. Often used for defence in depth, they were sometimes created in the front lines as at 'Manchester Hill' in 1918, which helped to blunt the German assault in March of that year.
Revetment	Reinforcing the walls of a trench to prevent collapse. Sandbags, wire netting and brushwood are common materials for revetment.
Salient	In general, any point in the line of defence which juts out towards the enemy. In castles, the 'salient angle' refers to the point of a bastion. In more general use, it can refer to a 'bulge' in the lines as in the Ypres Salient during the First World War.
Sangar	(Hindi). Originally a circular parapet of dry stone walling. In the First World War, it came to refer to any defences built above ground to avoid flooding. It remains in use today.
Sap	A trench extending forward of the front line. Originally, a means of moving a besieging force forward under cover. In the First World War, saps were frequently modified shell holes used as listening posts to give advance warning of enemy movements. Saps were a large part of military engineering hence the use of the term 'sapper' for a private soldier in the Royal Engineers.
Shell scrape	The most basic form of entrenchment. A shell scrape is a shallow hole dug in a temporary position for the purpose of sheltering from incoming fire. Usually just deep enough for the soldier to lie flat below ground level.
Traverse	A series of positions along the line of a trench, creating the cogged appearance of a castle wall laid on the ground. It is a buttress of earth at regular intervals along the length of a trench to maximize the field of fire, whilst also minimising the effect of an enfilade attack on any single point.
Work	Generic term for any defensive position.

BIBLIOGRAPHY

Adam-Smith, P. 1978 *The ANZACS*. Hamish Hamilton Ltd

Adkin, M. 2001 *The Waterloo Companion*. Aurum Press.

Adkins, R. 2004 *Trafalgar: Biography of a Battle*. Abacus Books

Ambrose, S. 1995 *D-Day: June 6th 1944, The Climactic Battle of World War II*. New York: Touchstone

Anderson, H. 2004 *How to Read a Trench Map*. Western Front Association Contributed Article. Available at www.westernfrontassociation.com

Anderton, M. 2002 Social space and social control: analysing movement and management on modern military sites. In Schofield J., Johnson, W.G. and Beck, C.M. (eds). *Matériel Culture: the archaeology of twentieth century conflict*. Routledge.

Balme, J. & Paterson, A. (eds). 2006 *Archaeology in Practice: A Student Guide to Archaeological Analyses*. Blackwell Publishing

Bilton, D. 2002 *The Trench: The Full Story of the 1st Hull Pals*. Leo Cooper

Binford, L.R. 1964 *A Consideration of Archaeological Research Design*. American Antiquity 29:425–41

Brighton, T. 2005 *Hell Riders*. Penguin

Brown, A. 1987 *Fieldwork for Archaeologists and Local Historians*. BT Batsford Books

Bryson, B. 2004 *A Short History of Nearly Everything*. Black Swan

Bull, S. 2003 *Trench Warfare*. Compendium Publishing

Burne, A.H. 1996 *The Battlefields of England* (Reprint of 1950 ed.). Penguin Classic Military History Series

Clarke, D. 2004 *The Angel of Mons: Phantom Soldiers and Ghostly Guardians*. Wiley

Cliffe, J.T. 1969 *The Yorkshire Gentry from the Reformation to the Civil War*. Athlone Press

Coles, J.M. 1979 *Experimental Archaeology*. Academic Press

Cooke, D. 2004 *The Civil War in Yorkshire: Fairfax versus Newcastle*. Leo Cooper Books

Cooksey, J. (ed.). 2005 *Battlefields Annual Review*. Pen & Sword Books

Corrigan, G. 2003 *Mud, Blood and Poppycock*. Cassell Books

Council for British Archaeology. 2002 *A Review of the Defence of Britain Project*. Available at www.britarch.ac.uk

Davis, W.C. (not dated) *The Civil War*. Salamander Books

De la Bédoyère, G. 2001 *Aviation Archaeology in Britain*. Shire Archaeology Series No80

Drewett, P.L. 1980 The Sussex Plough Damage Survey. In Hinchcliffe, J. & Schlada-Hall, R.T. (1980) *The Past Under the Plough*. Directorate of Ancient Monuments and Historic Buildings. DOE Occasional Paper No. 3: 69–73

Dyer, J. 2003. *Hillforts of England and Wales* (Revised Edition). Shire Archaeology Series No. 16

Fairclough, G. 2002. Archaeologists and the European Landscape Convention. In Fairclough, G. & Rippon, S. (eds) *Europe's Cultural Landscape: Archaeologists and the Management of Change*. Europae Archaeologiae Consilium Occasional Paper No. 2, 25–37

Fleming, P. 1957. *Operation Sea Lion*. New York: Simon & Schuster

Foard, G. 2001. The Archaeology of Attack: Battles and Sieges of the English Civil War. In Freeman, P.W.M. and Pollard, A. (eds) *Fields of Conflict: Progress and Prospect in Battlefield Archaeology*. Archaeopress.

Foard, G. 2004 *Field Offensive*. British Archaeology Issue 79 Nov. 2004: 10-14.

Foard, G. 2005 The Battle of Edgehill: History from the Field. In Cooksey, J (ed.) *Battlefields Annual Review* op cit.

Foot, W. 2002 *A Review of the Defence of Britain Project*. Council for British Archaeology.

Foot, W. 2003 *Public Archaeology: Defended Areas of World War II*. Conservation Bulletin 4, 8-11.

Foot, W. 2004 *Defence Areas: A national study of Second World War Anti-invasion Landscapes in England*. English Heritage

Fox, R.A. 1993 *Archaeology, History and Custer's Last Stand*. University of Oklahoma Press

Fraser, A. 2005 Finding Jakob. In Cooksey, J. (ed.) *Battlefields Annual Review*. Pen & Sword Books

Friar, S. 2003 *Sutton Companion to Castles*. Sutton Publishing

Gamble, C. 2005 *Archaeology: The Basics*. Routledge

Gane, M. 1999 Paul Virilio's bunker theorizing. *In Theory, Culture and Society* 16(5) 85-102

Gilling, M. 1984 *Place-names in the Landscape*. Dent

Grant, J. & Gorin, S. 2002 *The Archaeology Coursebook: An Introduction to Study Skills, Topics and Methods*. Fleming, N. Routledge Publishing

Griffiths, P. 2004 *Fortifications of the Western Front 1914-18*. Osprey Fortress Series No 24

Harrington, P. 2004 *English Civil War Archaeology*. B.T. Batsford Publishing

Hawkes, C. 1954 *Archaeological Theory and Method: Some Suggestions from the Old World*. American Anthropologist 56: 155-68

Hayward, J. 2002 *Myths and Legends of World War One*. Sutton Publishing

Hayward, J. 2003 *Myths and Legends of World War Two*. Sutton Publishing

Hegarty, C., Newsome S. & Winton, H. 2005 The Greatest Battlefield That Never Was: Suffolk Aerial Archaeology. In Cooksey, J. (ed.) *Battlefields Annual Review*. op. cit.

Hill, P & Wileman, J. *2002 Landscapes of War: The Archaeology of Aggression and Defence*. Tempus Publishing

Hinchcliffe, J. & Schlada–Hall, R.T. 1980 *The Past Under the Plough*. Directorate of Ancient Monuments and Historic Buildings. DOE Occasional Paper No 3: 69-73

HMSO 1911 *Manual of Field Engineering*. HMSO

Hockey, J. 1986 *Squaddies: Portrait of a Subculture*. University of Exeter

Hogg, I. 1975 *Fortress*. Macdonald Books

Hollowell, R. 1971 Aerial Photography and Fieldwork in the Upper Nene Valley. In Brown, A (ed.) *Bullettin of Northamptonshire Federation of Archaeological Societies*, 6

Holm, T. 1990 American Indian Veterans and the Vietnam War. In Capps, W (ed.) *The Vietnam Reader* (1990). Routledge

Holmes, R. 1995 *Riding the Retreat: Mons to the Marne Revisited*. Pimlico Books

Holmes, R. 2003 *Complete War Walks*. BBC Books

Holmes, R. 2004 *Tommy: The British Soldier on the Western Front 1914-1918*. HarperCollins

Hoskins, W.G. 1967 *Fieldwork in Local History*. Faber & Faber

Houlder, E. 2006 Think Before you Click. In British Archaeology, Issue 87 March/April 2006: 30

Jennings, C. & Weale, A. 1996 *Green-eyed Boys: 3 Para and the Battle for Mount Longdon*. HarperCollins

Johnson, D. 2003 *Adwalton Moor: The Battle that Changed a War*. Blackthorn Press

Johnson, R.U. & Buell, C. 1887 *Battles and Leaders of the Civil War.* New York

Jones, M. 2000 *The Making of the South Yorkshire Landscape: A Popular Guide to the History of the County's Countryside and Townscapes*. Wharncliffe Books

Kaufmann, J.E. & Kaufmann, H.W. 2003 *Fortress Third Reich: German Fortifications and Defense Systems of World War II*. New York: De Capo

Lacey, C. 2003 Fireshed: The application of GIS Techniques to Historic Military Data. Unpublished MSc dissertation, University of Southampton. In Schofield, J op cit.

Lewis, E. 1979 *Seacoast Fortifications of the United States*. Annapolis, Maryland: Naval Institute Press

Lock R. & Quantrill P. 2002 *Zulu Victory: The Epic of Isandhlwana and the Cover-up*. Greenhill Books

Lynch, T. 2003 Going Back Down South: The Falklands 2002. *Battlefields Review*, Issue 24: 38–45

Lynch, T. 2005 'Much blood has been spilt this year': The Battle of Tankersley Moor 1643. In Cooksey J. (ed.) *Battlefields Annual Review* op cit

Mahan, A.T. 1899 *Lessons of the War with Spain.* London: Sampson Low, Marston and Company

Marshall, S.L.A. 1947 *Men Against Fire.* New York: Wm. Morrow

McMillon, B. 1991 *The Archaeology Handbook: A Field Manual and Resource Guide.* New York: John Wiley & Sons

Museum of London. 2006 *The Archaeology of the Blitz.* Current Archaeology No 201: 486–92

Newark, T. 2002 *In Heroes' Footsteps: A Walker's Guide to The Battlefields of the World.* Silverdale Books

Oliver, N. 2005 *Not Forgotten.* Hodder & Stoughton

Osborne, M. *2004 Defending Britain: Twentieth Century Military Structures in the Landscape.* Tempus Publishing

Planel, P. 1995 *A Teacher's Guide to Battlefields, Defence, Conflict and Warfare.* English Heritage

Pollard, E, Hooper, M. & Moore, N. 1974 *Hedges (The New Naturalist).* Collins

Pollard, T. & Oliver, N. 2002 *Two Men in a Trench: Battlefield Archaeology – The Key to Unlocking the Past.* Michael Joseph

Pollard, T. & Oliver, N. 2003 *Two Men in a Trench II.* Michael Joseph

Pounds, N.J.G. 1992 *The Medieval Castle in England and Wales.* Cambridge University Press

Rackham, O. 1990 *Trees and Woodland in the British Landscape.* J.M. Dent

Rayner, M. 2004 *English Battlefields: 500 Battlefields that Shaped English History.* Tempus Publishing.

Saul, D. 2005 *Zulu: The Heroism and Tragedy of the Zulu War of 1879.* Penguin Books

Saunders, Andrew 1989 *Fortress Britain: Artillery Fortification in the British Isles and Ireland.* Beaufort Publishing.

Saunders, Anthony 2002 *Hitler's Atlantic Wall.* Sutton Publishing

Schofield, J. 2005 *Combat Archaeology.* Duckworth & Co.. Debates in Archaeology Series

Schwartz, H. 1984 Fear of the Dead: The Role of Social Ritual in Neutralizing Fantasies from Combat. In Schwartz, H (ed.) *Psychotherapy of the Combat Veteran.* Spectrum Publications

Scott, D.D., Fox R.A., Connor, M.A. & Harmon, D. 1989 *Archaeological Perspectives on the Battle of the Little Big Horn.* University of Oklahoma Press

Smurthwaite, D. 1984 *The Complete Guide to the Battlefields of Britain.* Michael Joseph Ltd

Sogndal, H. 2004 The Diggers' Quest to Locate the Fallen in Latvia. In *The Armourer*, Issue 61 Jan/ Feb 2004, 46–7

Stevens, J. 2002 *Foreword to British Battles: The Front Lines of History in Colour Photographs* by Guest, E. & K. English Heritage

Stocker, D. 1992 The Shadow of the General's Armchair. *Archaeology Journal* 149: 41–420

Sutherland, T. 2004 Topsoil: Key Battlefield Layer. *British Archaeology*, Issue 79 Nov 2004: 15

Sutherland, T. & Holst, M. 2005 *Battlefield Archaeology – A Guide to the Archaeology of Conflict.* Britsh Archaeology Jobs Resource November 2005. Available at: www.bajr.org/Documents/ BAJRBattleGuide.pdf

Swift, E. 2003 *Where They Lay: The Search for Those Who Fell in Battle and Were Left Behind.* Bantam Press

Tennant, P. 1992 *Edgehill and Beyond: The People's War in the South Midlands 1642-1645.* Alan Sutton Publishing

Thompson, M. 1991 *The Rise of the Castle.* Cambridge University Press

Trigger, B. 1989 *A History of Archaeological Thought.* Cambridge University Press

Valery, P. 1928 'On History'. In Regards sur le monde actuel. Quoted in Cohen, M.J. and Major, J. (eds) (2004) *History in Quotations.* Cassell Books

Van Emden, R. 2002 *The Trench: Experiencing Life on the Front Line 1916.* Bantam Press

Virilio, P. 1991 *Bunker Archaeology* (orig. 1975). Paris: Les Editions du Demi-Cercle

Wason, D. 2003 *Battlefield Detectives.* Granada Media

Wheeler, M. 1956 *Archaeology from the Earth.* Penguin

White, P. 2006 'Producing the Record'. In Balme, Jane and Paterson, Alistair (eds) *Archaeology in Practice: A Student Guide to Archaeological Analyses.* Blackwell Publishing

Whynne-Hammond, C. 1992 *Tracing the History of Place-names.* Countryside Books

Williams, G. 2003 *Stronghold Britain: Four Thousand Years of British Fortification.* Sutton Publishing

INDEX